THE LEVERAGE CODE

Build Position Before You Need It

MJ Carver

— — —

ISBN: 979-8-9954245-1-2
Imprint: MJ Squared Group

First Edition. Printed in the United States of America.
This book is designed to provide general information and perspective on the topics discussed. It is not a substitute for legal, financial, or other professional advice.

For permissions or inquiries, contact:
mjmj2222@gmail.com

Foreword

Leverage is often misunderstood.

In business, it is associated with debt.

In finance, it is associated with risk.

In negotiation, it is associated with power.

But in life, leverage is something quieter.

It is position.

It is the margin that lets you think clearly when others are panicking.

It is the insulation that lets you say "no thanks" when the pressure rises.

It is the discipline that builds options long before they are ever needed.

I did not learn this from a business school. I learned it the hard way — living close to the edge, watching what happened when disruption arrived and I had nothing behind me. And then, years later, watching what happened when it arrived again and I did.

The difference was not luck. It was not talent. It was not even income.

It was structure.

This book does not promise wealth.

It promises structure.

It does not offer shortcuts.

It offers positioning.

In the pages that follow, you will see leverage examined not as aggression, but as preparation. Not as dominance, but as insulation. Not as appearance, but as foundation.

If you read carefully — and apply deliberately — you will begin to feel something shift.

Less urgency.

Less dependence.

More clarity.

More choice.

Leverage is not luck.

It is engineered.

And to build it, you first need to see honestly where you stand.

Let's start there.

— — —

Dedication

To those building quietly — and those about to start.

May you always have options.

— — —

TABLE OF CONTENTS

Introduction: Leverage Is Position

I want to start with a moment.

Not a theory. Not a framework. A moment.

I was sitting at a desk late one evening, staring at a paycheck that looked fine from a distance. The number was solid. Respectable. If anyone had glanced at it, they would have thought: *he's doing okay.*

But by the time I'd run the math — rent, utilities, child obligations, debt, groceries — what remained was thin.

Not because I had been reckless.

Because I had been concentrated.

Everything depended on one source. One role. One deposit hitting every two weeks. And that deposit was doing everything: surviving, functioning, maintaining. It was not, however, creating options.

That is the distinction this book is built on.

Income is survival.

Position is something else entirely.

— — —

Most people think leverage is about power — titles, authority, wealth. The ability to demand things from others.

That is not what this book is about.

The leverage I am describing is quieter. It is the structural advantage that allows you to think clearly instead of reactively. To wait instead of concede. To say "no thanks" and mean it.

It is the difference between operating from need and operating from position.

When you operate from need — when one outcome determines your survival — you accept more than you should. You stay quiet when you should speak. You agree when you should pause. Not because you lack courage. Because you lack insulation.

I know this feeling intimately.

I have lived it twice. Once in my thirties, when I had almost nothing behind me and a job loss felt like free-fall. And again in my fifties — a layoff after five years with a company I had given everything to — when the hit was real, but the panic was not. Because by then, my wife and I had built something. Not a fortune. A cushion. Distance from the edge.

The difference between those two moments was not talent. It was not even effort.

It was structure.

— — —

This book is organized in two parts.

Part I is about seeing clearly. Before you can build leverage, you need to see where you are exposed — where you are fragile, where you are dependent, where you are operating from need. These are not comfortable questions. But they are necessary ones.

Part II is the build. Ten Codes. Ten structural principles that, applied consistently over time, reduce fragility and expand options.

You do not need to implement everything at once. Leverage is not built in a single decision. It is built in repeated, quiet ones.

One debt reduced.

One skill developed.

One month of expenses saved.

Each one invisible to the outside world.

Each one structural.

— — —

The world rewards appearance.

Life rewards stability.

Those are different things. And most people spend their energy on the wrong one.

This book is an invitation to stop building image and start building insulation.

To stop performing strength and start engineering it.

To stop chasing visible success and start constructing invisible leverage.

It is not glamorous work. It does not produce applause.

But it produces something better.

Options.

And options — real options, the kind backed by math and structure — are freedom.

Let's build.

— — —

PART I: Exposure & Awareness

Before you build leverage, you must see where you stand.

Most people do not lack intelligence.

They lack awareness of their exposure.

They work hard. They earn income. They maintain a lifestyle.

But they never measure position.

They never ask: Where am I fragile? Where am I dependent? Where am I operating from need?

Part I is not about solutions.

It is about honesty.

Because leverage is not built on motivation. It is built on honest assessment. You cannot strengthen what you refuse to examine. You cannot reduce fragility you refuse to acknowledge.

In these chapters, we will look at the invisible structures in your life. The power of saying "no thanks." The comfort that quietly erodes margin. The disruptions that reveal weakness. The dependence hidden in income. And the reality of your current leverage level.

This is not meant to discourage you.

It is meant to position you.

Because once you see clearly, you can build deliberately.

Chapter 1: The Invisible You

There was a season in my life when I lived close to the edge.

Not recklessly. Not because I was irresponsible or careless with money. Just close. Close enough that every deposit mattered. Close enough that every unexpected expense felt amplified. Close enough that uncertainty never fully left the room.

I was working hard. Physical work, demanding work — the kind that takes a toll on your body at the end of a long day. I pushed hard to prove I was valuable, to perform, to lead, to deliver. And by most external measures, I was doing exactly that.

I was competent.

With time and repetition, I got better. Processes became smoother. Decision-making became faster. Teams responded more efficiently. Problems got solved more quickly.

Competence compounds. I had seen that up close.

But the physical toll did not. Sore feet do not improve with repetition. Long days on your feet do not become easier because you have logged more of them. Fatigue does not compound like skill.

It accumulates. Quietly. Relentlessly.

And when you are operating from need — when you cannot afford to stop — you accept the toll without question. You push harder. Because you have no choice.

— — —

I remember one email in particular.

Late afternoon. Neutral subject line. Professional language about tightening expenses, evaluating staffing levels, aligning resources with performance goals.

Nothing personal. Nothing dramatic.

I read it twice. Then a third time.

Because when you live without margin, every cost-cutting memo feels personal.

Not emotionally. Mathematically.

If staffing is evaluated, roles are examined. If roles are examined, someone is unnecessary. If someone is unnecessary, someone is gone. And if income stops, bills do not.

That night I lay awake running the numbers. Rent. Utilities. Child expenses. Debt. Groceries.

I wasn't thinking about advancement or status.

I was thinking about survival.

That distinction matters.

When you live without margin, income is oxygen. You don't negotiate oxygen. You protect it. And protection changes everything about your posture — how you carry yourself, what you say yes to, what you tolerate.

You agree faster than you should.

You volunteer more than is healthy.

You overextend.

You stay quiet when you should speak.

Not because you lack courage.

Because you lack insulation.

— — —

That was the moment I understood something I had never been taught:

Hard work does not eliminate fragility.

You can be competent, trusted, respected — and still be exposed. Because leverage is not effort. Leverage is position.

There are two versions of you.

The visible version — your job title, your productivity, your lifestyle, your performance reviews, your outward confidence. This is what people measure.

And the invisible version — your savings, your reduced fixed costs, your discipline, your options, your ability to absorb disruption without panic. This is what protects you.

The visible version earns applause.

The invisible version earns stability.

Leverage lives in the invisible you.

When that email arrived, my visible self was strong. I performed well, led effectively, understood the work. But my invisible self was thin.

That is what mattered.

— — —

I am not writing this from a position of full insulation. I have not arrived somewhere comfortable and decided to look back with advice. I am still building. Just further from the edge than I once was.

The difference is not dramatic. It is structural.

I built savings — not large savings, but intentional savings. I paid off my car loan. Not because it was a headline moment, but because it removed a fixed obligation. One less automatic pressure. One less required payment. One less thing my income had to service before I had any say in it.

Those moves created distance.

And distance from the edge matters more than almost anything else.

The first few thousand dollars saved does not change your identity.

It changes your breathing.

You sleep differently. You think differently. You read corporate emails differently. Because the math behind your fear has shifted.

Margin reduces fear.

Reduced fear creates clarity.

Clarity strengthens decisions.

Better decisions compound.

— — —

Most people think leverage is dramatic — a large salary negotiation, a major business deal, a moment where power shifts visibly. It isn't. Leverage is built quietly.

One debt reduced.

One expense eliminated.

One skill learned.

One month of expenses saved.

Invisible moves. Uncelebrated moves. Unapplauded moves.

But structural.

Invisible strength does not signal status. It signals durability. And durability outlasts visibility.

Operating from need feels urgent.

Operating from position feels calm.

When you need the job, you accept quickly. When you need the deal, you concede early. When you need approval, you tolerate more. Need narrows vision. Position expands it.

That expansion is leverage.

You do not need to look powerful.

You need to be positioned.

— — —

Before we move on, sit with one question:

Where are you operating from need?

Where are you exposed? Where does your math create fear?

You cannot build leverage where you refuse to look.

The invisible you is not impressive at first. It is quiet. Disciplined. Intentional. It builds layers before it builds image. It reduces dependency before it increases lifestyle. It strengthens structure before it seeks recognition.

The world applauds visibility.

Life rewards stability.

When disruption arrives — and it will — you will not panic. You will steady yourself. And you will plan.

Because you built the invisible version of you before you needed it.

— — —

Reflection & Action

- Where in my life am I operating from need?
- What income, person, or lifestyle do I feel I cannot afford to lose?
- Where do I feel least confident — and is that confidence missing because of structure?
- What fixed obligation creates quiet pressure each month?
- If income stopped tomorrow, what would break first?

Action — Build One Layer

Do not overhaul your life. Build one layer. Choose one or two:

- Save your first $1,000
- Increase your emergency fund by one month of expenses
- Pay off one small debt
- Eliminate one recurring subscription
- Begin learning one portable skill

Small layers create distance.

Distance reduces fear.

Reduced fear increases leverage.

— — —

The Invisible You

What This Looks Like in Practice

Most people have never sat down and mapped their invisible self honestly. They know their visible numbers — salary, title, mortgage balance — but they have never written down the structural reality underneath.

Here is a simple exercise I call the Invisible Audit.

Take a piece of paper. Draw a line down the middle.

On the left side, write everything visible: your job title, your income, your car, your home, your lifestyle commitments. This is your public portfolio. The version of you that other people see and measure.

On the right side, write everything structural: your savings balance, your monthly fixed obligations, the number of months you could survive without income, your portable skills, your secondary income sources (if any), your debt situation.

Now look at both columns honestly.

Most people find the left column is full. The right column is thin.

That gap — the distance between your visible life and your structural reality — is your fragility score. The wider the gap, the more exposed you are. The narrower the gap, the more genuine leverage you possess.

The goal is not to eliminate the left column. It is to build the right column until it can support the left one — and then some.

When I did this exercise for the first time, the gap was alarming. My visible life looked reasonable. My structural reality was almost empty. I had no real savings. My skills were largely tied to one environment. My income came from one source. My fixed costs were high relative to what I earned.

I was performing stability I did not possess.

That audit changed how I thought about every financial decision I made from that point forward. Not dramatically — I did not overhaul my life overnight. But I started asking a different question before spending.

Not: *Can I afford this?*

But: *Does this widen the gap or close it?*

That question is the beginning of building the invisible you.

— — —

The Compounding Gap

There is something worth understanding about the gap between your visible and invisible self.

It compounds in both directions.

When you consistently make decisions that widen the gap — more visible spending, less structural saving — the gap grows faster than you expect. Comfort becomes expectation. Expectation becomes fixed cost. Fixed cost becomes dependency. And dependency becomes fragility.

But when you consistently make decisions that close the gap — even small ones — something shifts. The first month of savings feels minor. The second feels steadier. By the sixth month, your behavior starts to change in ways you did not plan for.

You read emails differently.

You enter conversations differently.

You make decisions differently.

Not because you have suddenly become wealthy. Because you have reduced the math of fear behind your choices.

Fear is the engine of poor decisions. Margin is the engine of good ones.

Every decision you make today is either building the invisible you — or eroding it.

There is no neutral ground.

— — —

Chapter 2: The Power of "No Thanks"

The first time I said "no" in a salary conversation, my heart was racing.

Not because I was angry. Because I was aware.

The offer wasn't insulting. It was reasonable. Competitive. Professionally framed. They walked through the budget constraints, mentioned internal equity, referenced performance metrics. It was the kind of offer many people would accept without hesitation.

And for a moment, I almost did.

Because I knew the math. I knew my obligations. I knew what landed in my account every two weeks and what left it. I felt the old version of myself surface — the version that calculated bills first, prioritized security over alignment, feared rocking the boat.

Say yes. Be grateful. Secure the income. Don't risk it.

That voice is loud when you operate from need.

But something had shifted. Not dramatically. Structurally.

I had savings. Not unlimited — but present. I had fewer fixed obligations than before. I had slightly more distance from the edge.

And that distance created space to think. Space between the offer and my response. Space between fear and decision.

So instead of saying yes, I said:

"Thank you. I appreciate the offer. I'll need some time to think about it."

Silence.

A few days later, I returned.

"This is close. But I'm going to have to say no at that number."

Not loud. Not aggressive. Not emotional.

Just steady.

No thanks.

— — —

I want to be clear about something. When I said "no" in that conversation, it wasn't reckless. It was calculated.

If the offer had been the only option, I would have accepted — and immediately begun positioning myself elsewhere. Not in desperation, but strategically. Because sometimes leverage is not about rejecting the offer. It is about refusing to remain dependent on it.

There are levels of "no."

An immediate no — when you have alternatives, and walking away is clean.

A conditional no — when you stay but negotiate better terms.

A delayed no — when you accept temporarily but reposition quietly, so that you're building toward the day you can leave on your own terms.

Each requires insulation. Without insulation, "no" is a bluff. With insulation, "no" is leverage.

— — —

Leverage in negotiation is rarely about dominance. It is about math.

If losing the deal puts you at genuine risk, you do not have leverage. If losing the deal is survivable, you do. That survivability — invisible, unannounced — is real power.

I saw this dynamic play out clearly in a moment at work years ago.

My boss walked out of a meeting and gave a direct instruction: I needed to work overnight shifts that weekend. No discussion. No negotiation. A directive.

I had children at home. My wife worked nights. I could not do it.

But this time, the math was different. I had savings. Enough to survive termination. Enough to search without panic. Not abundance — margin.

So I said: *"No thanks. I can't do that."*

Clearly. Without emotion. Without defensiveness.

My boss nodded and turned to a coworker.

Same request.

The coworker looked scared. Tense.

"Okay. I'll figure it out."

Two employees. Same request. Different posture.

The difference was not personality. The difference was not strength or weakness. The difference was position. My coworker was not incapable. They were simply not insulated. And when you cannot afford to lose the income, "no" disappears.

Managers sense this. Systems sense this.

Leverage is often felt before it is spoken.

— — —

There is another layer to "no thanks" that goes beyond the workplace.

Emotional leverage works the same way.

If you love someone and fear losing them to the point where you will accept things you shouldn't, your boundaries weaken. If you need approval, your standards lower. If you need a specific outcome, you concede before the conversation starts.

Need narrows vision. Leverage widens it.

That is why insulation matters beyond money. Emotional discipline is leverage. Self-respect is leverage. Clarity about what you will and will not tolerate is leverage.

The power of "no thanks" is not in the words.

It is in the math behind them.

Savings. Reduced fixed costs. Portable skills. Multiple income streams. Margin.

"No thanks" without structure is hope.

"No thanks" with structure is alignment.

— — —

Here is the firm truth:

If you cannot say no without fear, you are operating from need.

And if you are operating from need, you do not have leverage — regardless of how confident you appear on the outside.

Build margin.

Reduce dependency.

Increase options.

Then say "no thanks" calmly.

Because the most powerful words in negotiation are not loud.

They are steady.

— — —

Reflection & Action

- Where in my life do I struggle to say no?
- Is that struggle emotional — or structural?
- What outcome do I feel I cannot afford to lose?
- If I had six months of expenses saved, what would I decline immediately?
- Where am I agreeing out of fear rather than alignment?

Action — Strengthen Your "No"

Choose one or two:

- Increase your savings buffer
- Reduce one fixed obligation
- Begin building a second income stream
- Practice delaying agreement by 24 hours before committing
- Set one boundary this week where you normally overextend

The ability to say no is not personality.

It is preparation.

— — —

The Power of "No Thanks"

What This Looks Like in Practice

The ability to say "no thanks" is not a personality trait you either have or do not have. It is a skill — and like any skill, it can be developed through deliberate practice.

Here is the framework I use. I call it the Three-Layer No.

Layer One: The Structural No

This is the most powerful no. It is backed entirely by math. You can say no because the alternative is survivable. You have savings, options, or a second income stream that means walking away does not destabilize your life.

Building toward a structural no requires preparation before the conversation, not during it. You cannot engineer a structural no in the moment. You build it over months and years.

Ask yourself: In the most important negotiations in my life — salary, contracts, relationships, major commitments — do I have a structural no available to me? If yes, you have real leverage. If no, your work is clear.

Layer Two: The Conditional No

This is the negotiator's no. You are not walking away, but you are not accepting the current terms either. You are creating space for better terms to emerge.

"I appreciate the offer. I need to sit with this before I respond."

"I can work with this direction, but I need X adjusted before I can commit."

The conditional no requires less structural preparation than the structural no, but it requires emotional preparation. You need to be comfortable with silence, with uncertainty, with the discomfort of not immediately resolving tension.

Most people cannot do this because the silence feels dangerous. When you are operating from need, silence in a negotiation feels like the deal falling apart. When you are positioned, silence is simply space.

Layer Three: The Delayed No

This is the most underused form. You accept the current terms — but you begin immediately building the structural no so that next time, the conversation goes differently.

This is not weakness. This is strategy.

I have used this more than once. Accepted a situation I was not fully satisfied with, because I did not yet have the structural foundation to walk away cleanly. But I used that time to build. Reduced expenses. Built savings. Developed skills. Explored alternatives.

Six months later, the conversation was different. Not because I had become bolder. Because I had become more positioned.

———

A Scenario Most People Will Recognise

Consider a woman — we will call her Dana — who has been in the same role for four years. She is good at her job. Her manager knows it. But her salary has not kept pace with her value, and she knows it.

She asks for a meeting. Her manager acknowledges her contribution, explains budget constraints, and offers a 3% increase. Dana needs the income. She has two weeks of savings. Her fixed costs are high.

She accepts. Immediately. Without negotiation.

Now consider the same scenario — same woman, same role, same conversation — but Dana has spent the previous eight months quietly building.

She increased her savings to three months of expenses. She reduced two fixed costs. She developed a freelance skill that has already earned her $800 in side income. She has had two conversations with contacts at other companies.

She is not wealthy. She is not untouchable.

But she is positioned.

When her manager offers the same 3%, Dana pauses. She thanks him. She asks for time. She returns two days later.

"I appreciate the conversation. Based on what I'm seeing in the market and the value I'm bringing to this team, I was expecting something closer to 9%. Can we work toward that?"

Same woman. Same company. Same manager. Different outcome.

Not because Dana found courage she never had. Because she built structure that made courage possible.

— — —

Chapter 3: The Comfort Illusion

Comfort feels like stability.

It isn't.

Comfort feels like progress. Like reward. Like success. Like relief.

But comfort and position are not the same thing. And confusing the two quietly erodes leverage in a way that is nearly impossible to see until disruption reveals the damage.

— — —

There is nothing dramatic about most financial fragility. It does not arrive in a single crisis. It accumulates quietly.

One subscription. One upgraded plan. One daily habit. One convenience fee. One automatic renewal.

Individually, each one is harmless. Collectively, they are structural.

Fragility is rarely built in large decisions. It is built in repeated small ones.

I know this not from theory, but from experience. There were seasons when, after long days on my feet, exhausted and mentally stretched, the easiest decision was comfort. Convenience. A better meal. An upgraded option. Something that said: *you earned this.*

And sometimes that is fine. You work hard. You deserve to enjoy the results.

But repeated relief becomes routine. Routine becomes expectation. Expectation becomes entitlement. And entitlement competes directly with insulation.

The problem is not the individual decision. The problem is the pattern.

— — —

Modern companies understand this better than most consumers do.

The rewards app you downloaded is not casual. It is behavioral design.

You earn points. You unlock tiers. You see the message: *Only 150 points until Gold.*

That phrase is not accidental. It creates urgency without threat. It creates progress without actual progress. It creates loyalty without ownership.

You feel part of something. You feel ranked. You feel recognized.

So you spend to stay connected — not because you needed the product, but because you do not want to lose your place.

Here is the quiet inversion that most people miss:

You are chasing status with an airline while sacrificing position in your own life.

The rewards program increases the company's leverage. It creates predictable revenue, higher lifetime customer value, and a stronger position for the business.

But does it strengthen yours?

You trade cash flow for badges. Margin for tiers. Optionality for comfort.

You are not foolish. You are influenced. Repeatedly, subtly, and by design.

— — —

Comfort spending compounds differently than savings.

Savings compound in silence. Comfort compounds in expectation.

Once your lifestyle adjusts upward, it rarely adjusts downward easily. Comfort has inertia. And inertia increases fixed cost. Increased fixed cost reduces flexibility. Reduced flexibility reduces leverage.

Most people increase comfort before they increase insulation. They upgrade lifestyle before they build reserves. They reward themselves before they stabilize themselves.

Then disruption exposes the math.

Not because they were irresponsible. Because they were premature.

The better question is not: *Can I afford this?*

The better question is: *Does this strengthen my position?*

And if it doesn't — is it intentional, or automatic?

— — —

Here is the sharper truth.

Many people are fiercely loyal to brands. They track points. They know their tier status. They can recite loyalty benefits without hesitation.

But they cannot state how many months of expenses they could survive without income.

That imbalance matters.

Be loyal to your future first.

Let businesses earn your loyalty after your leverage is built.

You do not lose leverage in dramatic decisions. You lose it in engineered ones. In automatic renewals. In tier chasing. In comfort loops that feel like rewards.

If your comfort is growing faster than your margin, you are not building freedom.

You are building dependency — elegantly packaged.

Rewards feel like progress.

Margin is progress.

Choose the game that protects you.

— — —

Reflection & Action

- What subscriptions do I rarely use?
- What recurring expense feels small but compounds?
- What comfort habit is automatic rather than intentional?
- Am I more loyal to brands than to my own insulation?
- If I redirected one year of small comforts into savings, what would that total?

Action — Reclaim One Pattern

Choose one or two:

- Cancel one subscription
- Downgrade one recurring plan
- Replace one convenience expense with effort
- Redirect one "reward" expense into savings this month
- Book "just getting there" instead of upgrading

This is not deprivation.

It is repositioning.

— — —

The Comfort Illusion

What This Looks Like in Practice

The comfort audit is one of the most revealing exercises you can do — and one of the most uncomfortable.

For one month, track every non-essential expense. Not to judge yourself. To see the pattern clearly.

At the end of the month, categorise each item:

Intentional — you consciously chose it, you derived genuine value, you would choose it again.

Automatic — it happened without active decision. A subscription renewed. A habit triggered. A tier was maintained.

Emotional — you purchased because you were tired, stressed, seeking relief, or responding to a prompt (a notification, a sale, a points reminder).

Most people are surprised by how much of their spending falls into the automatic and emotional categories. Not because they are irresponsible, but because modern spending is engineered to bypass conscious decision-making.

The goal of this audit is not to eliminate spending. It is to make it deliberate.

Once you can see the automatic and emotional categories clearly, you can make one simple rule:

Before any non-essential purchase, pause for 24 hours.

That pause breaks the behavioral loop. It introduces friction. And friction creates intention.

For smaller amounts, 24 hours is enough. For larger amounts — anything that changes your monthly cash flow — extend that pause to a week.

You will find that a significant percentage of purchases simply disappear when given time to breathe. Not because you denied yourself. Because the urgency was manufactured, and manufactured urgency fades.

— — —

The Lifestyle Creep Timeline

Here is the pattern I have watched play out in my own life and in the lives of people around me.

Year one of a new income level: expenses increase modestly. Some genuine improvements. Some rewards. Reasonable.

Year two: the baseline has shifted. What felt like a reward in year one is now expected. Subscriptions that felt optional are now standard. The upgraded option is now the default.

Year three: any reduction feels like deprivation, even though the original baseline would have felt fine just thirty-six months earlier.

This is lifestyle creep. It does not feel dramatic in the moment. That is what makes it dangerous.

The antidote is not rigid frugality. It is conscious anchoring.

Once a year, ask: *What is my actual baseline? What could I remove without my quality of life genuinely suffering?*

Most people find the answer is more than they expected.

That gap — between what you could remove and what you actually remove — is leverage waiting to be built.

— — —

Chapter 4: Disruption & The Parachute

Divorce and relationship changes are not just emotional.

They are structural.

I remember looking at my paycheck after everything was divided. The number was the same as it had always been. But what it had to carry was different now.

Child support. Mortgage. Electric. Phone. Water. Insurance.

What remained after all of that felt thin. Not irresponsible. Not reckless.

Just thin.

I wasn't thinking about lifestyle. I wasn't thinking about dating, or travel, or the next chapter. I was thinking about the month. Could I cover it? What happens if something unexpected hits? What happens if the car needs work, or a medical bill arrives, or the hours at work change?

Divorce did not make me fragile. It revealed where I was already fragile.

That distinction matters more than it might seem.

— — —

There was another layer to it. Time.

I would not see my kids as often as I wanted. And when I did have time with them, I felt pressure — real pressure — to make it count. Take them somewhere. Do something memorable. Be present.

But "memorable" costs money. And money was already allocated before it arrived.

I could not even think about dating. Not emotionally — financially. Dinner felt irresponsible.

That is what disruption actually feels like. Not chaos. Compression.

Everything tightens. Options shrink. Every unexpected expense becomes amplified. Every delay feels threatening. Every repair carries weight.

Survival consumes energy. Positioning requires space.

And you cannot position from survival mode.

— — —

The deeper truth is this:

Disruption does not create weakness. It exposes structure.

Jobs change. Industries shift. Health fluctuates. Markets correct. Relationships end. Companies restructure. The only truly unpredictable thing about disruption is timing.

The question is not: *Will disruption come?*

The question is: *When it does, what will I have built to withstand it?*

I think about this in terms of a parachute.

You do not assemble and put on a parachute on the way down. You build it, check it, and put it on before you step out of the plane.

Savings. Reduced fixed costs. Portable skills. Multiple income streams. Health. Emotional discipline.

Each one a cord. Individually small. Collectively life-saving.

Most people attempt to build their parachute after they feel the drop. After the layoff. After the divorce. After the recession. After the diagnosis.

But fear narrows thinking. Desperation reduces options. And options are freedom.

— — —

There is a simple test that reveals your leverage level immediately:

If your primary income stopped tomorrow, what would happen?

Panic — or planning?

Your answer is structural. Not emotional. If the honest answer is panic, that is not weakness. It is information. And information allows design.

During the season following my divorce, I was not building leverage. I was reacting to exposure. Every decision was defensive. Every cost felt amplified.

That is what operating without a parachute looks like.

It is not dramatic. It is exhausting.

And it is entirely preventable — if you build before the drop.

— — —

Fragility is optional.

Disruption is not.

Reduce:

Single-source income. High fixed obligations. Lifestyle inflation. Dependency on one outcome.

Increase:

Margin. Skill portability. Revenue diversity. Health. Discipline.

Each layer strengthens the parachute. Each layer expands options. Each layer increases leverage.

You cannot control disruption. You can control preparation.

When disruption arrives, you will not rise to the level of your ambition.

You will fall to the level of your structure.

Build the structure now.

Because the fall is not the problem.

The absence of a parachute is.

— — —

Reflection & Action

- If my life divided tomorrow, what would break first?
- How many months could I operate without panic?
- What is my largest structural vulnerability?
- Where am I overly dependent on one outcome?
- What would I regret not building before disruption arrived?

Action — Add One Cord to the Parachute

Choose one or two:

- Add one month of expenses to savings
- Reduce one fixed cost permanently
- Begin building a secondary income stream
- Invest in a portable skill
- Strengthen one health discipline that increases resilience

Parachutes are built before the fall.

So is leverage.

— — —

Disruption & The Parachute

What This Looks Like in Practice

The Parachute Inventory is a structured way to assess how ready you are for disruption before it arrives.

Most people only discover their vulnerability after the drop. This exercise lets you see it clearly while you still have time to pack the parachute.

Rate each cord on a scale of 1 to 5 — where 1 means this cord does not exist yet and 5 means this cord is strong and tested.

Cord 1: Emergency Savings

How many months of essential expenses do you have saved?

0 months = 1. 1 month = 2. 2–3 months = 3. 4–6 months = 4. 6+ months = 5.

Cord 2: Income Diversification

Do you have any income beyond your primary source?

Nothing = 1. Occasional side income = 2. Small consistent secondary stream = 3. Multiple streams covering 25%+ of expenses = 4. Multiple streams covering 50%+ = 5.

Cord 3: Skill Portability

If your employer disappeared tomorrow, how quickly could you earn income elsewhere?

Months of searching = 1. Several months = 2. Weeks with effort = 3. Quickly in same industry = 4. Immediately across industries = 5.

Cord 4: Fixed Cost Flexibility

If your income dropped 30%, how quickly could you reduce expenses to match?

Impossible = 1. Very difficult = 2. Possible with sacrifice = 3. Manageable = 4. Easy — low fixed obligations = 5.

Cord 5: Health Resilience

Is your physical and mental health strong enough to absorb a high-stress disruption period?

Poor = 1. Struggling = 2. Average = 3. Strong = 4. Excellent = 5.

Add your scores.

5–10: Your parachute has significant gaps. Prioritise immediately.

11–16: Some cords exist. Focus on the weakest ones first.

17–21: Moderate preparation. Keep building deliberately.

22–25: Well prepared. Maintain and expand.

The purpose of this inventory is not to produce anxiety. It is to produce direction.

If you score a 1 or 2 on any cord, that is your next project. Not everything at once. The weakest cord first.

Because when disruption arrives, your parachute is only as strong as its weakest cord.

— — —

What Disruption Actually Looks Like Before It Happens

One thing I have learned from living through disruption more than once is that it almost always sends signals before it arrives.

The email with the careful language. The meeting that gets postponed twice. The reorganisation announcement that does not quite explain itself. The relationship that starts requiring more management than it used to.

Most people sense these signals and choose not to act on them. Not because they are foolish. Because acting on them requires confronting the possibility of disruption — and confronting that possibility feels more uncomfortable than ignoring it.

This is one of the most expensive mistakes you can make.

If you are sensing signals — trust them. Not to catastrophise. Not to panic. But to act.

Begin building the parachute when you sense the turbulence. Not after the drop.

I have made both mistakes. I have ignored signals and paid for it. And I have acted on signals — quietly, without drama — and found that the preparation changed everything about how I experienced what came next.

The disruption still came. The parachute made the difference.

— — —

Chapter 5: Revenue Streams & Fragility

Most people are one paycheck away from financial panic.

Not because they are reckless. Because they are concentrated.

If your rent, utilities, food, and obligations all depend on one deposit hitting your account every two weeks, that deposit carries enormous pressure. Remove it — and panic begins immediately.

That is not a character flaw. It is math.

Single-income dependency is fragile by design. When one employer provides 100% of your income, they hold structural leverage over you — regardless of how talented you are, how loyal you have been, or how well you perform.

Concentration amplifies exposure.

I lived this. There was a time when all of my financial weight sat on one source. One role. One salary. One structure. It looked stable from the outside.

It was simply uninterrupted.

Those are not the same thing.

Uninterrupted income feels safe — until it stops. True stability survives interruption.

— — —

Now imagine something slightly different.

Two revenue streams. Two deposits. Two sources.

You are not suddenly wealthy. But you are no longer one paycheck away from panic. You are half a paycheck away.

That difference matters more than it sounds. Because leverage is not about abundance. It is about reducing exposure. Even partial insulation changes posture. Even small diversification reduces fear. And reduced fear increases leverage.

Revenue diversification is not greed. It is insulation.

A second skill monetized. A side project that generates modest income. Consulting hours. Freelance work. Digital products. Investments that produce cash flow. It does not need to be dramatic.

It needs to exist.

———

Many people resist building additional streams because they feel tired. Too busy. Overextended. I understand that. There were seasons when the idea of doing anything beyond surviving the week felt impossible.

But disruption does not ask whether you feel ready. It arrives anyway.

And when it does, your existing structure is tested immediately.

If you have one source, your stress multiplies.

If you have two, your reaction stabilizes.

If you have three, you pivot.

This is not about becoming an entrepreneur overnight. It is about engineering resilience.

———

There is another layer worth understanding.

Income concentration affects negotiation in ways people rarely consider.

When your livelihood depends entirely on one stream, you tolerate more. You accept more. You hesitate to push back. Because the downside feels catastrophic. Every conversation where you might upset someone, every moment where you might be seen as difficult — it all carries weight it should not carry.

Diversification reduces catastrophic thinking.

And reduced catastrophic thinking improves every negotiation you will ever have.

— — —

Revenue streams should also be multi-use and adaptable.

If you build a side income, ask: Can this skill transfer across industries? Can this service evolve? Can this knowledge scale? Single-use income streams are still concentration.

The goal is not to juggle ten income streams. The goal is to reduce fragility.

One additional stream changes psychology.

Two changes posture.

Three changes power.

Move intentionally. Build slowly. Layer carefully. Protect margin. Diversify income. Reduce exposure.

Most financial panic is not caused by laziness. It is caused by concentration.

And concentration is a structural problem with a structural solution.

— — —

Reflection & Action

- What percentage of my income comes from one source?
- If that source paused for 60 days, what would happen?
- Do I have any secondary income stream — even small?
- What skill could I monetize within six months?
- Where am I concentrated without fully realizing it?

Action — Reduce Concentration

Choose one or two:

- Build a small secondary income stream
- Monetize one portable skill
- Invest in assets not tied to your employer
- Reduce one fixed expense to lower your required income threshold
- Allocate time weekly — even one hour — to developing alternative income

You do not need abundance.

You need insulation.

———

Revenue Streams & Fragility

What This Looks Like in Practice

Building a second income stream does not require a dramatic life change. It requires a specific question asked honestly:

What do I know how to do that someone else would pay for?

Most people underestimate the answer to this question. They assume it has to be something extraordinary — a unique talent, a proprietary skill, something no one else can offer.

It does not.

It has to be something useful to someone, delivered reliably.

Here is a simple framework for identifying your first or next income stream:

Step 1: Skills Inventory

Write down everything you do in your current role. Not just the headline — the actual tasks. Reporting. Training. Process design. Communication. Problem-solving. Managing up. Managing people. Systems. Analysis.

Then write down everything you do outside your role that has practical value. Organisation. Writing. Teaching. Cooking. Physical training. Technical troubleshooting. Research.

Most people fill half a page without trying.

Step 2: Market Filter

Look at each item and ask: Is there a market of people who need this and do not have it?

Not a massive market. Even a small, specific market is enough to generate supplemental income.

Step 3: Minimum Viable Start

Do not build a business. Build a first client, or a first product, or a first offer.

One consulting project. One piece of digital content. One freelance engagement. One service offered to one person.

The goal is not scale. The goal is proof of concept — and more importantly, proof that your income is not entirely dependent on one source.

— — —

The Psychology of the Second Stream

There is something that happens the first time a payment arrives from a source that is not your employer.

It is not about the amount. It could be $50. It could be $200. The amount is almost irrelevant in the early stages.

What changes is the feeling.

You realise, perhaps for the first time, that your earning ability is not entirely housed in one relationship. That your skills have value beyond one company's assessment of them. That your income — at least in principle — is not entirely at the mercy of one decision made by someone else.

That feeling changes posture.

I remember the first time I generated income outside my employer. It was modest. Genuinely modest. But I carried myself differently the next time I walked into a review conversation. Not because I was planning to leave. Because I knew, structurally, that I could.

That knowledge — backed by actual income, not just theory — is what changes behavior.

Build the second stream not for what it pays.

Build it for what it produces structurally.

Chapter 6: Your Leverage Level

By now, you understand something.

Leverage is not personality. It is not charisma or confidence or ambition.

It is structure. It is insulation. It is having options.

But understanding leverage is not the same as possessing it.

This chapter will ask you to measure honestly where you currently stand. Not to judge you. Not to discourage you. But because you cannot improve what you refuse to measure.

— — —

The Leverage Question

If your primary income stopped tomorrow — would you panic, or would you plan?

Pause before answering.

Your first honest reaction is the truth.

If the answer is panic, that is not weakness. It is exposure. Exposure is structural. And structure can be rebuilt.

Now we measure.

— — —

Financial Leverage

1. Emergency Margin

How many months of essential expenses could you cover without income?

- 0 months → Score: 1
- 1 month → Score: 2
- 2–3 months → Score: 3
- 4–6 months → Score: 4
- 6+ months → Score: 5

2. Fixed Cost Flexibility

How quickly could you reduce your monthly expenses if necessary?

- Impossible — most costs locked → Score: 1
- Difficult — minor reductions possible → Score: 2
- Moderate — some expenses adjustable → Score: 3
- Flexible — significant expenses reducible → Score: 4
- Highly flexible — low fixed obligations → Score: 5

Psychological checkpoint: If your margin is low and your fixed costs are high, you are not unlucky. You are concentrated. Concentration feels efficient until it breaks.

———

Revenue Leverage

3. Income Concentration

What percentage of your income comes from one source?

- 90–100% → Score: 1
- 75–89% → Score: 2
- 50–74% → Score: 3
- 25–49% → Score: 4

- Less than 25% → Score: 5

4. Skill Portability

If you lost your current role, how transferable are your skills?

- Highly specialized to one employer → Score: 1
- Limited outside current company → Score: 2
- Transferable within industry → Score: 3
- Transferable across industries → Score: 4
- Portable and independently monetizable → Score: 5

Psychological checkpoint: If one decision outside your control can eliminate your income, you are not secure. You are fragile. Fragility is not shame. It is information.

— — —

Emotional Leverage

5. Boundary Strength

Can you say "no" without fear of collapse?

- Rarely → Score: 1
- Sometimes → Score: 2
- Often → Score: 3
- Almost always → Score: 4
- Calmly and consistently → Score: 5

6. Outcome Dependence

How dependent are you on one specific outcome — one job, one relationship, one deal?

- Completely dependent → Score: 1
- Highly dependent → Score: 2

- Somewhat dependent → Score: 3
- Mostly independent → Score: 4
- Fully capable of walking away → Score: 5

Psychological checkpoint: If you cannot walk away, you do not have leverage. If you cannot decline without fear, you are operating from need. Need narrows vision. Leverage expands it.

— — —

Comfort Exposure

7. Lifestyle Inflation

Have your expenses increased as your income increased?

- Yes — significantly → Score: 1
- Yes — moderately → Score: 2
- Somewhat → Score: 3
- Minimally → Score: 4
- No — margin increased first → Score: 5

8. Loyalty vs. Position

Do you track reward points more closely than you track savings?

- Yes, always → Score: 1
- Sometimes → Score: 2
- Rarely → Score: 3
- Never → Score: 4–5

— — —

Health & Resilience

9. Physical Resilience

Is your body capable of absorbing stress and disruption?

- Poor condition → Score: 1
- Below average → Score: 2
- Average → Score: 3
- Strong → Score: 4
- Highly resilient → Score: 5

10. Mental Composure

How do you respond to unexpected financial stress?

- Immediate panic → Score: 1
- High stress → Score: 2
- Moderate stress → Score: 3
- Calm assessment → Score: 4
- Structured response → Score: 5

— — —

Your Leverage Score

Add your scores.

Minimum: 10 | Maximum: 50

- 10–20 → Highly Exposed
- 21–30 → Structurally Fragile
- 31–40 → Moderately Positioned
- 41–45 → Strongly Positioned
- 46–50 → Strategically Insulated

Do not inflate your score. Your future depends on accuracy, not comfort.

— — —

The Hard Mirror

If your score is low, that is not failure. It is clarity.

If your score is moderate, that is not arrival. It is progress.

If your score is high, that is not invincibility. It is responsibility — because leverage can erode quietly.

Most people never measure this. They assume stability because income arrives regularly. But income is not leverage.

Margin is leverage.

Options are leverage.

Position is leverage.

In Part II, we will break leverage down into clear, structural principles. Not motivation. Not hype.

Codes.

Because leverage is not accidental.

It is built.

And now you know where you stand.

— — —

Transition to Part II

Leverage runs beneath everyday life.

It shapes conversations, careers, relationships, and risk. Most people feel its effects. Few understand its mechanics.

In the chapters ahead, we will formalize those mechanics.

The Leverage Codes are not theory. They are structure.

And structure changes outcomes.

— — —

PART II: THE LEVERAGE CODES

You have seen your exposure.

You have measured your fragility.

You understand where you are positioned — and where you are not.

Now we build.

The Leverage Codes are not motivation. They are mechanics. Principles that reduce dependence, increase insulation, and expand options. Each Code strengthens structure. Each Code compounds over time.

You do not need to implement everything at once.

You need to build deliberately.

Leverage is not luck.

It is engineered.

The engineering begins now.

— — —

CODE 1

Leverage Is a Force Multiplier

Two employees work equally hard.

One negotiates a 15% increase. The other accepts the initial offer.

Same effort. Different outcome.

Two business owners operate in the same industry. One relies on a single client for 70% of revenue. The other has five clients, evenly distributed. A recession hits. One panics. One adjusts.

Same market. Different exposure.

Two parents face a job loss. One has six months of savings. The other has two weeks. Same disruption. Different stress level.

— — —

Leverage is not effort. It is amplification.

It is the force that multiplies outcome relative to input. A small structural advantage can produce disproportionate strength. A small structural weakness can produce disproportionate damage.

In physics, a lever allows a small force to move a heavy object. In life, leverage allows a small position to move a large outcome.

The person who can walk away has leverage. The person who cannot is leveraged.

The difference may be a savings account. Or a skill. Or a second income stream. Or emotional independence.

Small structures. Large consequences.

— — —

Most people misunderstand leverage. They think it is power.

Power is visible — title, authority, wealth.

Leverage is different. Leverage is the application of position to produce outsized results. Power can exist without leverage. But leverage is what makes position useful.

A CEO has power. An employee with a competing offer has leverage.

A landlord has power. A tenant with savings and alternatives has leverage.

Leverage is rarely loud. It is structural.

— — —

Leverage also works negatively — and this is critical to understand.

Debt is financial leverage. When used wisely, it amplifies gain. When used poorly, it accelerates collapse.

Emotional dependence is leverage. It can deepen connection — or distort boundaries.

Single-source income is leverage. It amplifies stability until it amplifies risk.

Leverage multiplies. It does not discriminate. It magnifies whatever structure exists.

This is why leverage must be intentional. If you do not build it consciously, you inherit it passively. And inherited leverage is almost always fragile.

— — —

Here is the critical shift:

Most people try to increase effort. Few increase leverage.

They work longer. Push harder. Accept more. Add responsibility. Chase visibility.

But effort without structure does not multiply. It exhausts.

Leverage multiplies. That is why two people with similar intelligence and work ethic can produce dramatically different outcomes over a lifetime. One built position. One built effort.

Ask yourself: Where is my force multiplied? Where is it diminished? If I apply energy here, does it compound — or drain?

Leverage appears in negotiation, income structure, time control, emotional boundaries, skill portability, and financial insulation. Small advantages in each area compound across a lifetime.

You do not need massive leverage to change outcomes.

You need strategic leverage.

A single additional income stream. Three months of savings. One portable skill. Reduced fixed costs. Clear emotional boundaries.

Each one small. Each one a multiplying force.

— — —

Your Leverage Level

Reading Your Score Honestly

When I first created this assessment for myself, I scored a 19.

Highly Exposed.

Not because I lacked income. Not because I was financially illiterate. Because I had never sat down and measured the structural reality of my life against the questions that actually matter.

That score was uncomfortable. It was also the most useful piece of information I had received in years.

Here is what I want you to understand about your score, whatever it is.

A low score is not a verdict. It is a starting point.

Most people who read this book and complete this assessment honestly will score somewhere between 15 and 32. Most people are structurally fragile in at least two or three areas, often without realising it — because income has continued arriving and disruption has not yet arrived to reveal the gaps.

The purpose of the assessment is not to make you feel behind. It is to show you exactly where to build next.

Take your lowest two scores. Those are your priorities for the next six months.

Not everything. Not an overhaul. Two areas. Focused improvement. Measured progress.

Come back to the assessment in six months and run it again. Your score will have moved. And watching your score move — watching the structure you are building show up as real numbers — is one of the most motivating experiences this process produces.

———

The Scores That Most Often Surprise People

In my experience — both from my own assessment and from sharing this framework with others — two categories consistently produce the biggest surprises.

Emotional Leverage.

Most people rate themselves higher on Boundary Strength and Outcome Dependence than the reality supports. It is uncomfortable to acknowledge that you are staying in a situation because you fear the alternative, or that you struggle to say no consistently. So the honest score gets inflated.

I encourage you to answer these two questions particularly carefully.

Ask yourself: in the last three significant situations where I could have said no — a work request, a social obligation, a financial commitment — did I say yes because I genuinely wanted to, or because the discomfort of no felt too large?

If the honest answer is the latter, your Boundary Strength score is probably lower than you initially rated it.

Comfort Exposure.

The lifestyle inflation question is another area where people tend to round up. Yes, expenses have increased — but moderately, not significantly. The points tracking is casual, not a real driver of spending.

Here is a useful test: look at your subscription list and calculate the total monthly cost. Look at your dining and convenience spending over the last 90 days. Compare both to what they were three years ago.

For most people, the increase is not moderate. It is significant.

Rate yourself based on what the numbers say, not what the feeling suggests.

— — —

The Multiplier You Are Already Using Against Yourself

Most people understand leverage as something to build.

What they miss is that they are already using it — against themselves.

Every high fixed obligation you carry is leverage working in reverse. Your mortgage, your car payments, your subscriptions, your lifestyle commitments — these are all force multipliers applied to your income. They take your earnings and multiply the speed at which they disappear, leaving you with less margin, fewer options, and reduced negotiating power.

This is negative leverage. And it compounds just as efficiently as positive leverage does.

Consider two people who both earn $75,000 per year.

Person A has $4,200 in monthly fixed obligations — rent, car payments, loan repayments, subscriptions, insurance. That is 67% of their monthly take-home income committed before they have any discretionary say.

Person B has $2,100 in monthly fixed obligations — lower rent, no car payment (paid off), minimal subscriptions. That is 34% of their monthly take-home income committed automatically.

Same earnings. But Person B has more than twice as much discretionary margin each month. Over a year, that margin compounds into savings, into options, into structural leverage that Person A simply cannot build at the same pace.

Person A is experiencing negative leverage working efficiently against them.

Person B has reduced the negative multiplier — and is now able to build positive leverage with the margin that creates.

The first step in building leverage as a force multiplier is not adding new structures.

It is removing the structures already multiplying against you.

— — —

The Audit That Changes Everything

Here is the most clarifying 30-minute exercise in this book.

Open your bank statement for the last 60 days.

Go through every outgoing transaction and categorise it as one of three things:

Building — this expense directly increases your leverage. Savings contributions. Debt repayments. Skill development. Investments.

Sustaining — this expense maintains necessary life function. Rent, utilities, groceries, essential transport.

Consuming — this expense produces no lasting structural benefit. Subscriptions, dining upgrades, comfort purchases, tier maintenance, impulse spending.

Now add up each category.

Most people find that their Consuming category is significantly larger than their Building category. Often dramatically so.

The gap between those two numbers is leverage that is being spent rather than built.

You do not need to eliminate the Consuming category. You need to consciously choose its size — not let it grow automatically while Building stays thin.

Even moving 10% of Consuming into Building changes the trajectory of your position over 12–18 months.

This audit is the most direct path from where you are to where leverage multiplies.

— — —

Reflection & Action

- Where does my effort currently produce minimal return?
- Where does small preparation create large benefit?
- What single structural improvement would multiply my outcomes?
- Am I relying on effort where I should be building leverage?

Action — Identify One Multiplier

Choose one or two:

- Build one income stream that compounds
- Reduce one dependency that amplifies risk
- Develop one skill that increases earning flexibility
- Increase savings to create negotiating leverage
- Set one boundary that protects your energy

Leverage is not built accidentally.

It is engineered.

— — —

Leverage Is a Force Multiplier

What This Looks Like in Practice

Understanding leverage as a force multiplier is one thing. Identifying where your specific leverage points are — and where they are not — requires a different kind of thinking.

Here is a practical framework called the Leverage Map.

Draw four quadrants on a piece of paper.

Top left: High Effort, Low Return

Work that consumes significant time and energy but produces limited outcomes. Most people have more here than they realise. Long hours in roles where their contribution is undervalued. Relationships that drain without reciprocating. Commitments that produce obligation but not progress.

Top right: High Effort, High Return

Work that is demanding but genuinely multiplying. Where skill, positioning, and preparation combine to produce disproportionate results.

Bottom left: Low Effort, Low Return

Passive activity that neither drains nor builds. Acceptable in small doses. Dangerous as a default.

Bottom right: Low Effort, High Return

This is where leverage lives. The income stream that runs with minimal maintenance. The skill that opens doors across industries. The savings buffer that changes every negotiation. The reduced fixed cost that permanently lowers your required income.

The goal is to move as much of your time and energy from the top left into the top right and bottom right quadrants.

Most people are heavily concentrated in the top left. They are working hard, but not strategically. They are generating effort without generating leverage.

The question is not: *How do I work harder?*

The question is: *Where does my effort multiply most?*

Identify your top two activities in the bottom right quadrant — things already working with minimal input — and invest in expanding them before adding anything new.

— — —

The Multiplier in Real Time

A man I know — a mid-level manager in a logistics company — spent years trying to advance through effort alone. He worked longer hours than anyone on his team. He volunteered for every project. He earned good reviews.

But his income barely moved. His negotiating position never changed. His lifestyle required everything he earned, which meant every review conversation was conducted from need.

He was multiplying effort. He was not multiplying leverage.

Over eighteen months, he made three structural changes.

He paid off his car — removing $480 in monthly fixed obligations.

He started consulting two evenings per week in his area of expertise — generating a modest but consistent secondary income.

He developed a certification in a complementary skill that made him portable across three adjacent industries — not just his current one.

None of these changes were dramatic. Individually, each seemed minor.

But together, they shifted the math of his life.

His next review conversation was different. He negotiated a 12% increase — not because he had become more aggressive, but because the cost of not getting it had changed structurally. He could absorb a no. His manager sensed it.

Same person. Same company. Different leverage.

— — —

CODE 2

Position > Power

Position is greater than power.

Power is visible. Position is structural.

Power is loud. Position is quiet.

Power commands attention. Position controls outcome.

— — —

A CEO has power. An employee with multiple offers has position.

A wealthy partner may appear powerful. The partner who can leave calmly has position.

A manager can demand compliance. The employee who can walk away negotiates differently.

Power can pressure. Position can choose.

Choice is stronger.

— — —

Power depends on authority. Position depends on insulation.

Power can disappear with title loss. Position remains when structure is intact.

In business, power often comes from hierarchy — title, ownership, control of resources. But position is built differently. Cash reserves. Low dependency. Skill portability. Market alternatives.

Negotiating leverage does not come from shouting louder. It comes from needing less.

— — —

In relationships, power often appears emotional. One person may earn more. One person may initiate conflict or withdraw affection.

But position is something else entirely.

The person who is emotionally independent. The person whose self-respect is anchored in identity, not approval. The person who can leave without collapsing.

That person has position.

Position does not threaten. It steadies.

— — —

There is a reason the calmest person in the room often holds the most leverage. They are not operating from urgency. They are not negotiating from fear. They are not reacting from need.

They are positioned.

Power without position is fragile. Position without visible power is durable.

A loud executive with high lifestyle inflation and single-source income may have visible power — and zero structural leverage.

A quiet professional with margin, diversified income, and portable skills may appear ordinary — and possess real leverage.

Do not confuse visibility with insulation.

— — —

Here is the psychological truth:

People who rely on power fear losing it. People who build position do not panic when power shifts.

Because power is external. Position is internal.

Power can be granted. Position must be built.

Many people chase power before building position. They chase title before insulation. Income before margin. Recognition before resilience. And when power shifts — as it always does — they collapse under the weight of their own exposure.

Position first. Power later.

— — —

Position is built through:

Savings. Reduced fixed costs. Multiple income streams. Portable skills. Emotional discipline. Physical resilience.

None of these look impressive on social media. All of them create leverage.

Test your position with these questions:

If this person walked away, would I destabilize?

If this employer terminated me, would I panic?

If this deal fell through, would I collapse?

Your answers reveal your structure.

You do not need to look powerful. You need to be positioned.

Power seeks dominance. Position creates freedom.

Freedom is leverage.

— — —

The Position You Build In Relationships

Position matters in every kind of relationship — not just professional ones.

I want to address this directly because it is the area where people most often resist the concept.

The idea of building "position" in a personal relationship can feel cold. Transactional. Like you are approaching intimacy with the mindset of a negotiator.

That is not what this means.

Position in a relationship is not about leverage over another person. It is about not being leveraged by your own fear of losing them.

There is a difference between two kinds of relationship stability.

The first is stability built on choice. You are in this relationship because you genuinely want to be. Because the person adds to your life, aligns with your values, and makes the partnership worth investing in. You could leave — structurally, emotionally, practically — but you choose not to. That choice is real, and it strengthens the relationship.

The second is stability built on dependency. You stay not entirely by choice, but because the alternative — being alone, financial disruption, loss of the lifestyle the relationship enables, fear of starting over — feels more threatening than the dissatisfaction you experience within it. You stay because you cannot afford, in some concrete sense, to leave.

The first kind of stability produces healthy, reciprocal relationships.

The second produces anxiety, resentment, and boundaries that erode over time.

Building position in a relationship means ensuring that you are choosing it, not trapped in it.

This requires:

Maintaining financial independence — not identical finances, but your own income and savings.

Maintaining emotional resilience — friendships, interests, and identity that exist beyond the relationship itself.

Maintaining self-respect — clear understanding of what you will and will not accept, and the structural ability to act on that understanding if necessary.

None of this is in conflict with deep love, genuine commitment, or full investment in a partnership. Position does not make you distant. It makes your presence genuine.

— — —

When Power Shifts

Here is something I have observed across many professional environments.

Power shifts. Always. It is not a question of whether but when.

The executive who seemed untouchable gets restructured out. The manager whose approval felt essential moves to another company. The client who represented 60% of revenue makes an unexpected decision. The relationship that felt permanent ends.

When power shifts, the people who relied on it collapse with it.

The people who built position independently of it do not.

I have watched this play out more than once in my own career. Environments I thought were stable turned out to be built on personalities, not structures. When the personalities changed, so did the environment. The people who had cultivated portable skills, external relationships, financial insulation — they navigated the shift. The people who had built their security entirely inside the power structure scrambled.

This is not cynicism. It is pattern recognition.

Build position that does not depend on any single power structure remaining intact.

Your skills should not live entirely inside one organisation.

Your income should not depend entirely on one decision-maker.

Your identity should not be housed entirely in one environment.

Position is portable.

Power is not.

— — —

Reflection & Action

- Where am I mistaking power for position?
- What visible success do I rely on that lacks structural insulation?
- If I lost my title tomorrow, what would remain?
- In what relationship am I negotiating from need rather than strength?

Action — Build Position Quietly

Choose one or two:

- Increase savings before increasing lifestyle
- Develop one portable skill outside your current employer
- Reduce one fixed obligation that increases dependency
- Strengthen one boundary in a relationship
- Build one alternative option before you need it

Power fades.

Position compounds.

Build what lasts.

— — —

Position > Power

What This Looks Like in Practice

The Position Audit is a structured exercise that helps you identify where in your life you are operating from position — and where you are operating from power that lacks structural backing.

Answer these questions honestly:

In my career:

- If my employer terminated me tomorrow, how long before I would panic?
- Do I have skills that are valued outside this company — not just within it?
- In my last negotiation, was I operating from position or from need?

In my finances:

- Does my lifestyle depend on my income continuing without interruption?
- If my income dropped 25%, would I have to make immediate, painful changes?
- Am I building margin, or maintaining appearance?

In my relationships:

- Am I in key relationships because I choose to be — or because I fear the alternative?
- Do I hold boundaries consistently, or do I adjust them based on what I think others need from me?
- If a significant relationship ended, would I destabilize — financially, emotionally, structurally?

In negotiations:

- Do I typically accept the first offer or the initial terms?
- Do I feel pressure to resolve tension quickly, even at the cost of a better outcome?
- When someone applies pressure, do I tend to concede or hold?

There are no right answers here — only honest ones.

The areas where you notice the most discomfort are the areas where your power is most visible and your position is most thin.

That is where to build next.

— — —

The Quiet Professional

I want to come back to something I touched on in Part I — the idea of the quiet professional.

In every organisation I have worked in, there has been a version of this person. Someone who does not announce their position. Does not signal their options. Does not broadcast their leverage.

They simply hold steady.

In meetings where others compete for visibility, they contribute precisely. In negotiations where others rush to resolve tension, they wait. In moments where others react, they pause.

At first, this can look like passivity. Like disengagement. Like someone who is simply not ambitious.

But watch long enough and the pattern emerges.

These people get what they negotiate for. They exit situations cleanly when exits are necessary. They are not particularly concerned with what others think of them, because their security is not housed in others' opinions.

They are positioned.

The irony is that this kind of person often accumulates more actual power over time than those who chase it aggressively. Because position compounds. Power without position erodes.

The goal is not to become cold or strategic in a calculating way. It is simply to ensure that your stability is backed by structure — not performance.

When your security comes from what you have built rather than what others think of you, everything changes.

— — —

CODE 3

Reduce Fragility First

A man I once worked with drove a beautiful luxury SUV.

Premium trim. Custom wheels. Immaculate condition.

He worked hard, earned well, and felt he deserved it. He did deserve it — by every measure. He had built a strong career and a visible life.

Until the company restructured.

The announcement came quickly. Budget cuts. Department consolidation. Positions eliminated.

He wasn't reckless. He wasn't incompetent. He was concentrated.

Within thirty days, his income stopped. But his payments did not.

SUV. Mortgage. Credit cards. Insurance. Private school tuition.

Everything had been built on continuation — on the assumption that income would keep arriving. Not on insulation. On uninterrupted flow.

He didn't need a raise. He needed margin.

That distinction came too late.

— — —

Growth without insulation creates fragility.

Many people focus on increasing income. Few focus on reducing exposure. They chase expansion. They ignore vulnerability. But fragility multiplies faster than growth, because fragility is structural.

Most financial stress does not come from low income. It comes from fixed commitments tied to that income. High fixed obligations amplify disruption. Low fixed obligations absorb it.

That is leverage.

If your income grows and your fixed costs grow with it, you are not building leverage. You are scaling exposure. That is lifestyle inflation. It feels like success. It functions like fragility.

— — —

Reducing fragility is not glamorous. It does not produce applause.

No one congratulates you for eliminating a payment. No one posts about lowering recurring expenses.

But every reduced obligation increases flexibility. Flexibility increases options. Options are freedom.

Consider two professionals earning identical salaries. One spends most of it. The other spends 60% and saves 40%. A disruption hits. One negotiates calmly. One negotiates desperately.

Same income. Different fragility.

— — —

Here is the structural principle:

Before you try to increase upside, reduce downside.

Before you try to scale income, reduce dependency.

Before you chase growth, reduce exposure.

This is not pessimism. It is engineering.

Fragility hides in: single-source income, high fixed debt, lifestyle commitments, emotional dependence, poor health, and lack of skill portability. Each one amplifies disruption. Reduce one, and your leverage increases immediately.

There is a psychological resistance to this Code. Reducing fragility feels like shrinking. Like playing small. Like holding back.

But the opposite is true. You are not shrinking.

You are stabilizing. And stability multiplies future opportunity.

— — —

Many people want more power. Few want less fragility.

But fragility determines your ceiling.

You cannot negotiate boldly with a high burn rate. You cannot walk away with maximum dependency. You cannot build leverage while structurally exposed.

Reduce fragility first. Then build.

The uncomfortable truth is this: some people look successful but are structurally fragile. Others look ordinary but are quietly insulated. When disruption arrives, the roles reverse.

Reducing fragility is the fastest path to increasing leverage.

Build upward slowly. Build downward aggressively. Strengthen the base. Then expand.

Because leverage compounds best on stable ground.

— — —

The Hidden Fragility of Success

One of the most counterintuitive truths about fragility is that it tends to increase as visible success increases — unless you are deliberately managing the gap between the two.

Here is why.

As income grows, lifestyle tends to grow with it. This is natural. You earn more, you spend more. You upgrade housing, transportation, experiences. You make commitments that reflect the income level you have reached.

None of this is wrong.

But each upgrade creates a new fixed floor for your lifestyle. And that floor determines how much disruption you can absorb.

The person earning $50,000 with $2,500 in monthly fixed costs can absorb significant disruption. Their required income is low relative to what is available.

The person earning $200,000 with $12,000 in monthly fixed costs — a common ratio among high earners — has a fragility profile that most people would not expect from someone at that income level. Their required income is extremely high. A significant disruption would be immediately severe.

High income with high fixed costs is not security.

It is fragility with better aesthetics.

The most financially secure people I have encountered in my life are not always the highest earners. They are the people who have maintained the widest gap between their income and their fixed obligations — regardless of what income level they have reached.

They built lifestyle more slowly than they built margin.

And that sequencing — margin before lifestyle, insulation before expansion — is the discipline that creates genuine security at any income level.

— — —

Three Questions Before Any Major Financial Commitment

Before committing to any significant ongoing financial obligation — a new lease, a car purchase, a new subscription tier, a lifestyle upgrade of any kind — I run three questions.

Question 1: What does this add to my monthly fixed floor?

Every commitment increases the minimum income you require to function without disruption. Know this number before you commit. Add it to your existing Fixed Obligation Ratio and assess whether the new ratio still allows adequate margin.

Question 2: What would I have to give up if income dropped 30%?

Run the disruption scenario before it is hypothetical. If your income dropped significantly tomorrow, would this commitment survive the cut — or would it be the first thing that created crisis?

Question 3: Am I adding this because it builds my life, or because it maintains a performance of my life?

This is the honest question. Some commitments genuinely improve your quality of life. Others maintain a social or professional image you have constructed. The second category deserves far more scrutiny than the first.

If a commitment survives all three questions, make it with confidence.

If it fails any one of them, reconsider whether the timing is right.

— — —

Reflection & Action

- What is my single largest fixed obligation?
- What percentage of my income is committed before it arrives?
- Where am I scaling lifestyle instead of margin?
- What would destabilize me fastest?

Action — Remove One Weak Point

Choose one or two:

- Pay off one high-interest debt
- Reduce one recurring expense permanently
- Delay one lifestyle upgrade
- Increase your savings rate before increasing spending
- Build one skill that reduces income dependence

Fragility shrinks leverage.

Stability expands it.

Reduce fragility first.

— — —

Reduce Fragility First

What This Looks Like in Practice

The Fragility Reduction Plan is a 90-day focused exercise designed to identify and eliminate your highest-impact vulnerabilities.

Week 1–2: The Fragility Audit

List every fixed financial obligation you carry. Every one.

Mortgage or rent. Car payment. Insurance. Subscriptions. Loan repayments. Regular commitments that recur monthly regardless of your income.

Add them up.

Now divide that number by your monthly take-home income.

If more than 60% of your income is committed before you have any say in it, you are operating with structural fragility. If it is above 70%, disruption would be severe.

This number is your Fixed Obligation Ratio. Write it down. It is your starting point.

Week 3–4: Identify the Top Three

From your list, identify the three fixed obligations that:

- Cost the most relative to their value to you
- Could be reduced or eliminated fastest
- Carry the highest emotional weight when you think about losing income

These are your priority targets.

Week 5–8: Execute One Reduction

Choose the most accessible of the three and take one concrete action to reduce it.

Cancel a subscription. Refinance a loan. Sell an asset that carries monthly cost. Negotiate a lower rate on an existing service.

One reduction. Real and immediate.

Week 9–12: Build the Buffer

Redirect the freed-up cash flow into a dedicated savings account. Not a general account — a specific one labelled for what it is: your insulation fund.

Even one month of expenses in a dedicated account changes how you think about disruption.

The goal of these 90 days is not transformation. It is proof of concept — proving to yourself that structural change is possible, and that small reductions compound into real leverage.

— — —

The Fragility Paradox

Here is something most people find counterintuitive:

The people who look most financially successful are often the most fragile.

High income. High fixed costs. High lifestyle commitments. No margin.

The person earning $200,000 a year with a $9,000 monthly fixed obligation is structurally more fragile than the person earning $80,000 with a $2,500 monthly commitment.

One disruption and the high earner is in immediate crisis. The lower earner has breathing room.

This is the fragility paradox: income creates the illusion of security while the spending it enables creates the reality of exposure.

I have been on both sides of this in different seasons of my life. The season when income was highest was not the season I felt most secure. It was the season my fixed costs had grown to match — and sometimes exceed — what was coming in.

Security is not income.

Security is the gap between income and obligation.

Build the gap deliberately.

— — —

CODE 4

Invisible Strength Wins

On a work trip years ago, a small group of us traveled together.

Long days. Meetings. Events. Team dinners in the evening.

One of the colleagues on that trip was quiet. Polite. Professional. Reserved. The unspoken assumption — shared among most of us without anyone saying it — was that she probably went back to her hotel room each night, watched television, ordered room service, kept to herself.

She didn't talk about investments. She didn't mention side projects or businesses. She didn't signal lifestyle. She simply showed up, did the work, and said very little beyond what was required.

A few days into the trip, she mentioned she was bored one afternoon.

She went out on her own.

That evening, some of us were walking along the beach near the hotel.

And there she was — cruising past in a rented motorboat. Champagne in hand. Calm. Unbothered. Not performing. Not seeking acknowledgment.

She didn't wave. She didn't explain. She simply enjoyed.

It turned out she had built a substantial side business while working full-time. While appearing ordinary. While saying very little.

— — —

Meanwhile, most of us on that trip knew something else was true. Every dinner. Every round of drinks. Every "I'll just put it on my card."

The spending on that trip was pushing toward a credit limit for more than one person. We would spend the next few months paying off what had felt like harmless indulgence.

She would not.

That was the difference.

No signaling. No boasting. No social proof.

Just position.

— — —

The world applauds visibility. Life rewards stability.

Many people project success. Few build insulation.

The quiet colleague had not withdrawn socially. She had positioned financially. She did not need validation. She had options. And options change posture in ways that are impossible to fake.

Invisible strength is often underestimated — right up until the moment it is not.

Think of a smaller person walking down a dark street who has trained in martial arts for ten years. They appear unimposing. The larger person approaching may feel confident. Until preparation reveals itself.

Invisible preparation creates surprise. Surprise creates advantage. Advantage is leverage.

— — —

Most people focus on visible signals. Title. Car. Clothing. Vacation. Status.

But visible signals can be financed. Invisible strength must be built.

There is a reason some people remain calm during disruption. They are not reacting in real time. They prepared long before. Savings. Skill development. Revenue diversification. Reduced dependency.

None of it glamorous. All of it structural.

Invisible leverage compounds quietly.

The first thousand dollars saved feels small. The second feels steadier. The third changes breathing. By the time others notice your stability, the structure was built years earlier.

— — —

Here is the mistake many make: they try to look positioned before they are positioned.

They increase lifestyle before insulation. They increase visibility before stability. They project strength before building it.

Projection without insulation is performance.

Insulation without projection is power.

The colleague in the motorboat did not need to signal success. Her posture was different — unhurried, unafraid, unburdened. She did not measure purchases or calculate indulgence or worry about timing.

Because margin removes urgency. Urgency exposes fragility.

— — —

Invisible strength also builds a specific kind of confidence. Not loud confidence. Calm confidence.

The kind that allows you to say "no thanks." The kind that allows you to negotiate patiently. The kind that allows you to wait.

Confidence built from position is different from confidence built from ego. One collapses under pressure. One steadies.

Build what cannot be seen.

Reduce what increases exposure.

Strengthen what compounds silently.

The world may not notice.

But disruption will.

— — —

Reflection & Action

- What parts of my life are visible but fragile?
- What invisible structures have I built?
- Where am I signaling strength instead of building it?
- If disruption hit tomorrow, would my invisible structure hold?

Action — Build in Silence

Choose one or two:

- Increase savings before increasing lifestyle
- Build a second income stream quietly
- Invest in a portable skill without announcing it
- Reduce one fixed obligation without replacing it with another
- Strengthen physical health consistently and privately

You do not need applause.

You need insulation.

Invisible strength wins.

— — —

Invisible Strength Wins

What This Looks Like in Practice

Building invisible strength requires a deliberate shift in what you optimise for.

Most people optimise for what others see. This is natural — social approval is a powerful driver, and the feedback loops are immediate. You upgrade your car, people notice. You display a title, people respond. You signal lifestyle, people affirm.

But invisible strength requires optimising for something that produces no immediate social feedback.

Here is a simple principle I call the Delayed Visibility Rule:

Build for six months before you show for one.

This means: for every visible upgrade or lifestyle improvement you want to make, spend the preceding six months building structural insulation of equivalent or greater value.

Want to upgrade your car? Spend six months increasing savings by the equivalent of the payment first. Then upgrade — from a position of strength rather than desire.

Want to take the premium vacation? Spend six months building a small secondary income stream first. Let that stream pay for it, not your primary income.

Want to invest in an expensive course or certification? Build three months of expenses first. Then invest in the skill from a position of stability.

This is not deprivation. It is sequencing.

The visible things still happen. They just happen after the invisible foundation has been laid. And that sequencing —

building before displaying — changes the structural reality of your life over time.

— — —

What Invisible Strength Produces Over Time

I want to be direct about something.

Invisible strength is lonely in the short term.

When you are reducing expenses while others are upgrading, it can feel like falling behind. When you are building quietly while others are signalling loudly, it can feel like invisibility is the same as failure.

It is not.

What invisible strength produces over time is a quality that is almost impossible to manufacture artificially:

Steadiness.

The person who has built genuine insulation — not performed it, but actually built it — carries themselves differently. They are not louder. They are not more aggressive. They are not particularly impressive to look at.

But they are steady.

They do not panic when disruption arrives. They do not collapse when pressure rises. They do not concede in negotiations when they should hold.

Because their security is structural, not performative.

I have watched this play out across careers, relationships, and financial situations. The people who age best — professionally and personally — are almost always the ones who chose invisible strength over visible performance in the years when the choice was hardest.

The colleague in the motorboat was not the loudest person on that work trip. She was the steadiest. And steadiness, over time, is the most powerful asset a person can carry.

CODE 5

Income Is Survival. Margin Is Leverage

I remember staring at my paycheck one night after the divorce.

The number was solid. Respectable. If you had looked at it from the outside, you would have thought: *he's doing fine.*

But the gross number was not the number that mattered.

Child support. Mortgage. Electric. Phone. Water. Insurance. Groceries. Fuel.

By the time those automatic withdrawals cleared, what remained was thin.

Not irresponsible. Not reckless.

Just thin.

The paycheck was survival. But it was not leverage.

— — —

Income keeps the lights on. Margin determines whether you can breathe.

Those are different things.

You can earn well and still be fragile. You can earn moderately and be insulated. The difference is not income. It is what remains after obligations.

Many people chase income. Few calculate margin.

Income is impressive. Margin is quiet.

Income is visible. Margin is structural.

Income earns applause. Margin earns leverage.

— — —

There was a time when every dollar had a destination before it arrived. Rent, utilities, obligations — it was all choreography. If one expense increased, something else had to shrink. If income paused, panic would begin immediately.

The paycheck sustained life.

It did not create options.

— — —

Two people can earn the same salary.

One spends 95% of it.

One spends 60% and saves 40%.

On paper, they look equal.

In structure, they are not even close.

One is one paycheck away from panic. The other is building insulation every month.

Over time, the gap widens. Not because of income. Because of margin.

When my margin improved — even slightly — my behavior changed. I did not need a dramatic raise. I needed breathing room. And breathing room created leverage.

It allowed me to say no calmly. To wait. To reposition. To think longer-term.

That is the multiplier effect of margin.

— — —

Here is where many people get trapped.

They increase income — and immediately increase lifestyle. New car. Better apartment. Higher subscriptions. More visible comfort.

Income rises. Margin stays flat.

They feel successful. But structurally, nothing changed. The paycheck grew. The leverage did not.

Margin requires restraint. Restraint requires discipline. Discipline creates optionality. Options are freedom.

Margin often feels like deprivation in the short term. You drive the older car. You skip the upgrade. You delay the vacation.

It does not feel glamorous.

But margin accumulates power quietly. And once it reaches a certain threshold, something shifts. You are no longer negotiating from survival. You are negotiating from position.

— — —

Many people say: *I just need to earn more.*

Maybe.

But often the more urgent question is: *What percentage of my income becomes margin?*

Because income without margin is motion.

Margin creates direction.

Income is necessary. Margin is powerful. Build both.

But build margin deliberately.

— — —

The Three Margins

Most people think of margin as a single number — what remains after expenses.

But there are actually three distinct margins worth tracking, each of which tells a different part of the story.

Financial Margin

This is the one most people are familiar with — the gap between income and spending. The number that tells you how much is being built versus consumed each month.

Track this monthly. Express it as a percentage of income. Build it deliberately.

Time Margin

This one is less discussed but equally important.

Time margin is the gap between your committed time — your job, your obligations, your fixed social and family commitments — and your discretionary time. Time you control. Time available for rest, skill development, second income building, or simply thinking.

People with no time margin are as fragile as people with no financial margin. They have no capacity to respond to opportunity or disruption. Every new demand on their time creates crisis.

Protect your time margin as deliberately as you protect your financial margin.

Energy Margin

Energy margin is perhaps the most overlooked of the three.

It is the gap between your current energy output — physical, mental, emotional — and your maximum sustainable capacity.

When energy margin is low, decision quality drops. Patience shrinks. Emotional regulation suffers. The ability to think long-term — which is the foundation of all leverage-building — diminishes.

Building energy margin requires attending to sleep, physical health, and the emotional weight you are carrying. It requires reducing energy drains — relationships, environments, and commitments that consume more than they restore.

The best financial decisions are made from positions of energy surplus, not energy depletion.

All three margins feed each other. Financial margin reduces the stress that depletes energy margin. Energy margin improves the quality of decisions that build financial margin. Time margin creates the space for both.

Build all three.

— — —

Margin as a Competitive Advantage

There is a professional dimension to margin that most people miss entirely.

When you have financial, time, and energy margin, you are able to do something that most of your professional peers cannot:

You can say yes to the right opportunities rather than the urgent ones.

Most people operate at or near capacity across all three dimensions. When an opportunity arrives — a new project, a business idea, a professional development investment, a relationship worth cultivating — they cannot engage with it properly because they have no margin to absorb it.

The person with margin can.

They can take on the project. Explore the idea. Make the investment. Spend the time.

Over a career or a business, the compounding effect of being able to say yes to the right things — rather than defaulting to whatever is urgent — is enormous.

Margin is not just protection from downside. It is access to upside.

Build it for both reasons.

— — —

Reflection & Action

- What percentage of my income becomes margin?
- If income stopped for 60 days, what would happen?
- Am I increasing lifestyle faster than margin?
- What fixed obligation reduces my breathing room most?

Action — Strengthen Margin

Choose one or two:

- Increase your savings rate by 5%
- Direct one future bonus or raise entirely toward margin
- Eliminate one fixed cost permanently
- Delay one lifestyle upgrade for 12 months
- Track margin monthly, not just income

Income sustains you.

Margin positions you.

Build margin. Build leverage.

— — —

Income Is Survival. Margin Is Leverage

What This Looks Like in Practice

The Margin Tracking System is the most practical tool in this book. It is simple, takes less than ten minutes per month, and will tell you more about your real financial position than any budget app.

Here is how it works.

At the end of each month, record three numbers:

Number 1: Total Income

Everything that came in. Primary salary, any side income, any irregular income.

Number 2: Total Fixed Obligations

Everything that left automatically. Rent, mortgage, loan repayments, insurance, subscriptions, child support, anything that recurs regardless of your decisions.

Number 3: Margin

Income minus Fixed Obligations, minus essential variable expenses (groceries, utilities, fuel). This is what remained as genuinely discretionary.

Now calculate your Margin Percentage: Margin ÷ Income × 100.

If your Margin Percentage is below 10%, you are in survival mode. One missed deposit and panic begins.

If it is between 10–20%, you have minimal insulation. Disruption would be stressful but survivable short-term.

If it is 20–35%, you are building genuine leverage. This range, sustained for 12–18 months, produces real options.

Above 35%: you are positioning strongly. This is the zone where leverage compounds most effectively.

Track this number monthly. Not income — margin.

Most people track income because it feels good. Tracking margin is what changes behaviour.

— — —

The Margin Conversation Nobody Has

I want to tell you about a conversation I never had with anyone when I was younger — and wish I had.

Nobody taught me to track margin. Nobody explained the difference between income and leverage. Nobody sat down and said: the number on your paycheck is not your financial position. Your financial position is the gap between what comes in and what is already spent before you touch it.

I learned this the hard way, through a season of compression after my divorce when that gap was almost nothing. When I watched colleagues earning less than me appear far more stable, and I eventually understood why.

They had built margin. I had built lifestyle.

The education system teaches you to earn. Very few people are taught to position.

This book is trying to give you the conversation I never had.

Track margin. Build margin. Protect margin.

Not income. Not lifestyle. Not appearances.

Margin is the number that tells the truth about where you stand.

— — —

CODE 6

Options Are Freedom

Freedom is misunderstood.

Most people define it emotionally. Doing what you want. Going where you want. Buying what you want.

That is lifestyle.

Freedom is structural.

Freedom is the ability to choose without fear of collapse.

If you cannot choose, you are not free. If you cannot decline, you are not free. If you cannot walk away, you are not free.

Options create freedom. And options are built — not granted.

— — —

A person with one job and no savings is not free. They may feel stable. But they are structurally dependent.

A person with savings, portable skills, and multiple revenue streams may not appear wealthy. But they possess options. And options change everything about how you carry yourself, how you negotiate, and how you respond to pressure.

Money is not about luxury. It is about optionality.

Consider this: if your employer reduced your pay by 20% tomorrow, what would you do? Accept quietly? Panic? Or negotiate calmly?

Your answer depends entirely on options.

— — —

In relationships, options matter — not to threaten, not to manipulate, but to stabilize.

If you are with someone because you choose them, that is strength. If you are with someone because you fear being alone, that is dependence.

Choice strengthens connection. Need distorts it.

When you have alternatives, everything shifts. You wait longer. You negotiate better. You tolerate less. You think more clearly. You respond instead of react.

That is leverage.

— — —

Many people do not lack talent. They lack options.

They stay in roles they dislike. They tolerate treatment they resent. They accept compensation below their value.

Not because they are weak. Because their structure limits them.

Options are not personality. They are preparation.

Options are built through savings, low fixed costs, revenue diversification, skill portability, health, and emotional discipline. Each layer expands the field of choice.

— — —

Here is the test:

What can you decline without destabilizing your life?

If the answer is "very little," your work is clear.

Build options.

Options are not built overnight. They are accumulated — layer by layer, margin by margin, skill by skill, income stream by income stream, reduced obligation by reduced obligation.

Small expansions compound.

One option is survival.

Two options are leverage.

Three options are strength.

Freedom is not about escape. It is about choice.

And choice is built.

— — —

The Option You Have Not Considered

Most people, when they think about building options, focus on the obvious ones.

A different job. A side income. More savings. A different living situation.

These are important. But there is a category of option that is even more powerful and far less discussed:

The option to wait.

In most negotiations and decisions, the person who can afford to wait holds more leverage than the person who must decide immediately. Patience — real patience, backed by structural insulation — is one of the most powerful options you can possess.

Consider a job offer. The person with two months of savings must decide quickly. Their urgency is visible. The interviewer senses it. The leverage flows toward the employer.

The person with eight months of savings can take their time. They can explore other opportunities. They can negotiate more thoroughly. They can decline an offer that does not meet their criteria without panic.

The option to wait is not a passive option. It is an active structural advantage.

Building the option to wait requires: adequate savings, reduced urgency, low enough fixed costs that the absence of income is survivable for the required waiting period.

Before your next significant decision — a job change, a major purchase, a business decision, a relationship commitment — ask: Do I have the option to wait? And if not, what would it take to build it?

— — —

Options You Can Build This Month

I want to make this concrete. Here are options that are genuinely buildable within 30 days, regardless of your starting position.

The Information Option

Reach out to two or three people in roles or industries adjacent to yours. Not to job hunt — simply to maintain active relationships that expand your professional visibility and awareness.

This costs nothing except 30 minutes per person. But it builds an option: when a transition becomes necessary, you have active relationships rather than starting from cold.

The Knowledge Option

Identify one skill that would increase your portability and commit to 30 minutes per day developing it. Thirty days of deliberate practice at something specific creates genuine incremental capability.

This is a small option, but it is real. And real options compound.

The Financial Option

Open a dedicated savings account — separate from your main account, harder to access casually — and transfer any amount into it. Even $100. Even $50.

This is not about the amount. It is about creating the structure of financial optionality. An account that exists is something you can build on. The psychological reality of having started changes how you think about building further.

The Clarity Option

Write down three things you would change about your current situation if the financial and practical constraints were removed.

This exercise clarifies what you actually want, separate from what you feel constrained to. And clarity about what you want is a prerequisite for building the options to pursue it.

Options do not require grand gestures. They require consistent, small, intentional actions taken in a specific direction.

Start today. With one.

— — —

Reflection & Action

- What can I not walk away from right now?
- Why?
- How many months of savings would meaningfully expand my choices?
- What skill would give me an alternative income source?
- Where am I staying because I have no real option?

Action — Expand One Option

Choose one or two:

- Build three months of expenses in savings
- Begin developing a monetizable skill
- Reduce one fixed obligation that limits mobility
- Build one alternative income stream
- Strengthen one boundary that protects autonomy

You do not need to look powerful.

You need options.

Options are freedom.

Build them.

— — —

Options Are Freedom

What This Looks Like in Practice

The Options Inventory is a structured way to measure — honestly — how many real options you currently have in the key areas of your life.

Rate yourself from 1 to 5 in each area:

Career Options

1 = I have one job and no real alternatives

2 = I have one job but some transferable skills

3 = I could find another role within 1–3 months

4 = I have active professional relationships and could move quickly

5 = I have multiple income sources and could replace primary income if needed

Financial Options

1 = One paycheck away from crisis

2 = One month of savings

3 = Three months of savings and reduced fixed costs

4 = Six months of savings, some secondary income

5 = Multiple income streams, low fixed obligations, strong reserves

Relationship Options

1 = Completely dependent on one relationship for stability/identity

2 = One primary relationship with minimal external support

3 = Strong primary relationship and some external anchors

4 = Diversified emotional anchors, strong self-reliance

5 = Relationships of choice, not dependency

Skill Options

1 = Skills tied to one employer or one industry

2 = Some transferability within current sector

3 = Skills transferable across industries

4 = Skills independently monetizable

5 = Multiple skill sets generating income across environments

Add your scores. Maximum is 20.

5–8: Options are severely limited. This is the highest priority area to address.

9–12: Some options exist. Build deliberately in the weakest area first.

13–16: Moderate optionality. Continue building.

17–20: Strong position. Maintain and expand.

The value of this inventory is not the score. It is identifying which single area, if addressed, would most improve your overall position.

Focus there first.

— — —

The Freedom Test

Here is a test worth running periodically — perhaps once a year.

Sit quietly and ask yourself, honestly: *If I could change one major thing in my life right now — a job, a relationship, a living situation, a commitment — what would it be?*

Most people can answer this question immediately. The answer is often something they have known for a while.

Now ask the second question: *What is preventing me from making that change?*

If the honest answer involves fear of financial collapse, loss of income, inability to survive the transition — that is a structural problem. And structural problems have structural solutions.

The purpose of building options is not to make changes recklessly. It is to ensure that the changes you choose to make are made from choice rather than from constraint.

Freedom is not doing whatever you want. Freedom is not being trapped by what you fear losing.

Build the options. The decisions become clearer when fear is removed from the equation.

— — —

CODE 7

Having Options Requires Discipline

"Only 150 points until Gold."

You open the app.

You weren't planning to buy anything. But you are close. Close to a tier. Close to something that feels like progress, like recognition, like a reward you have almost earned.

You scroll. You calculate. If you book the premium flight instead of the budget one, you will hit the threshold. If you upgrade the hotel, you will earn double points. If you just spend a little more, you will lock it in.

It feels strategic. It feels smart. It feels earned.

But it is temptation dressed as optimization.

— — —

Having options requires discipline.

Because options shrink quietly — not through catastrophe, but through micro-decisions.

Each indulgence is small. Each upgrade is rationalized. Each comfort is justified. Individually harmless. Collectively erosive.

You do not lose leverage in dramatic collapses. You lose it in incremental surrender.

Lifestyle inflation. Subscription creep. Reward chasing. Comfort loops.

Each one reduces margin. Reduced margin reduces options. Reduced options reduce freedom.

— — —

The most powerful "no" you will ever say is not to your boss.

It is to yourself.

No to the upgrade. No to the impulse. No to the visible reward.

Not because you cannot afford it. Because you are building something greater.

Discipline is misunderstood. It is not punishment. It is protection.

It protects margin, flexibility, future choice, and negotiating power.

Without discipline, options collapse under comfort.

— — —

Consider two people who both receive a raise.

One increases savings. One increases lifestyle.

Five years later, one has insulation. The other has expectation.

Same income increase. Different discipline. Different leverage.

— — —

Temptation is strongest when you are tired. After long workdays. After stressful conversations. After emotional strain. Comfort feels deserved.

And sometimes it is.

But repeated indulgence compounds expectation. Expectation becomes habit. Baseline becomes fixed cost.

Fixed cost reduces flexibility. Flexibility is leverage.

— — —

There is a deeper psychological layer here.

When you resist immediate gratification, you are not just saving money. You are strengthening identity.

You are reinforcing: *I do not operate from impulse. I build before I display. I protect future freedom.*

That identity compounds.

Discipline is the invisible engine behind leverage.

Without it, margin evaporates, options narrow, and fragility grows quietly. With it, margin compounds, options expand, and position strengthens.

Most people want freedom. Few want restraint. But restraint creates freedom.

— — —

Ask yourself before the next decision:

Does this increase my options — or reduce them?

If it reduces them, is it intentional or reactive?

That single question can change the trajectory of a decade.

Having options is not built once. It is maintained — daily, through decisions that no one applauds.

That is discipline.

And discipline protects leverage.

— — —

The Decision You Make Before the Temptation

The most effective form of discipline is not resisting temptation in the moment.

It is making the decision before the temptation arrives.

This is a principle from behavioural psychology that has significant practical applications to building leverage.

When you are calm, well-rested, and not under any immediate pressure, your decision-making is at its best. Your long-term thinking is clearest. Your ability to weigh future consequences against present desire is strongest.

When you are tired, stressed, emotionally depleted, or facing real-time social pressure — your decision-making is at its worst. Your brain defaults to what feels good now rather than what builds structure over time.

The discipline strategy that works is: make your most important financial and structural decisions when you are at your best, in advance, and then make them automatic so that the depleted version of you does not get to override them.

Practically, this means:

Set up your savings transfer as an automatic deduction before payday — not a manual transfer you decide to make after you have already seen the money in your account.

Set your budget categories before the month starts — not reactively after spending has already happened.

Set your decision rules before you enter negotiations or high-pressure situations — what you will accept, what you will not, and what will trigger a walk-away.

The prepared version of you is smarter than the pressured version. Let the prepared version make the rules. Let the system enforce them.

— — —

What Discipline Looks Like at Different Income Levels

A common misconception about financial discipline is that it becomes easier as income increases. That with more money, the temptations become easier to resist because the stakes of any single decision feel smaller.

The opposite is often true.

As income increases, so does the scale of temptation. The car upgrade becomes a different car, not the absence of a car. The subscription becomes a premium tier. The dining upgrade becomes a different category of restaurant.

The discipline required at $100,000 per year is not easier than the discipline required at $50,000 per year. It is different — higher stakes, more socially reinforced, more systematically marketed to.

The people who build leverage most effectively across income levels are not those with the most willpower. They are those who have built systems that make disciplined behaviour the default — regardless of the level of income flowing through them.

Build the system when income is lower. The habits you establish now will determine how you handle income when it grows.

Discipline applied at $60,000 per year builds the architecture for leverage at $150,000 per year.

Discipline ignored at $60,000 typically produces fragility at $150,000.

— — —

Reflection & Action

- Where do I rationalize upgrades?
- What recurring indulgence reduces margin?
- Do I increase lifestyle faster than insulation?
- What identity am I reinforcing through my spending patterns?

Action — Strengthen Discipline

Choose one or two:

- Delay one non-essential purchase by 30 days
- Direct one upcoming raise entirely into savings
- Cancel one subscription you barely notice
- Set a fixed savings percentage before spending, not after
- Track lifestyle inflation annually

Freedom is not accidental.

It is protected.

Having options requires discipline.

— — —

Having Options Requires Discipline

What This Looks Like in Practice

Discipline is not a character trait you have or lack. It is a system you build or fail to build.

Here is the Discipline Architecture — a set of structural guardrails that make disciplined financial behaviour automatic rather than willpower-dependent.

Guardrail 1: Pre-committed Savings

Before your income hits your spending account, route a fixed percentage to a separate savings account automatically. Not what is left over — a fixed percentage off the top.

Start at 5% if that is all that is currently possible. The amount matters less than the habit. Over time, increase to 10%, then 15%, then 20%.

The key is automation. Willpower is finite. Systems are not.

Guardrail 2: The 48-Hour Rule

Any non-essential purchase above a threshold you set — perhaps $50, perhaps $100 — waits 48 hours before you buy it.

This single rule eliminates a significant percentage of emotional spending without requiring ongoing vigilance. The urgency that drove the desire either persists after 48 hours (in which case it may be a genuine need) or it dissipates (in which case it was manufactured).

Guardrail 3: Annual Lifestyle Audit

Once a year, sit down and ask: What have I added to my regular spending this year that was not there last year? Is each addition intentional — or did it accumulate automatically?

Remove what is automatic and unexamined. Retain what is intentional and valued.

Guardrail 4: The Raise Protocol

Every time your income increases — a raise, a bonus, a side income payment — allocate the first 50% to margin before lifestyle. The second 50% can improve lifestyle.

This is the single most effective way to prevent lifestyle creep while still allowing life to improve over time.

— — —

Discipline as Identity

There is a deeper reason discipline matters beyond the financial mechanics.

The decisions you make repeatedly become your identity.

If you consistently choose immediate gratification over future security, you are reinforcing an identity — whether you intend to or not — of someone who does not build. Someone for whom the present is always worth more than the future.

If you consistently choose structure over comfort, you are reinforcing a different identity. Someone who builds deliberately. Someone whose future self matters as much as their present self.

This is not about self-punishment or rigid austerity. It is about intention.

Every time you pause before spending. Every time you redirect a raise into savings. Every time you say no to the upgrade and yes to the margin — you are casting a vote for a specific kind of person.

And those votes accumulate.

Not quickly. Not dramatically. But over time, the person those votes have been building shows up in negotiations. In conversations. In the steadiness with which you carry disruption.

Discipline is not what you deny yourself.

It is what you build for yourself.

— — —

CODE 8

Diversification Reduces Dependence

"Don't put all your eggs in one basket."

Most people hear that phrase and think about money. Investments. Stocks. Retirement accounts.

But diversification is not just financial. It is structural.

Any time your stability depends on one source — one income, one identity, one person, one skill — you are exposed. Concentration feels simple.

It is fragile.

— — —

Imagine carrying all of your eggs in one basket. You hold it carefully. You protect it. You move slowly.

Because if it drops, everything breaks.

Now imagine carrying five baskets. If one falls, the others remain.

That is diversification. Not excess. Resilience.

— — —

Most people diversify too late. After the disruption. After the loss. After the collapse. But diversification is not reaction. It is preparation.

Income is the obvious example. If one employer provides 100% of your income, that employer holds structural leverage over you. If you have multiple revenue streams, the dynamic shifts. You negotiate differently. You think differently. You tolerate less. Not because you are aggressive. Because you are distributed.

But money is only one basket.

Many people place their entire identity in one role.

I am my job. I am my title. I am my income.

When that role disappears, stability disappears with it.

Diversified identity protects you. You are more than one role, more than one title, more than one environment. That breadth creates leverage.

— — —

Relationships can become a single basket too.

If one person is your only emotional support, your only companion, your only source of affirmation, the relationship carries enormous pressure it was not designed to carry. Pressure distorts balance.

Diversified emotional anchors — friendships, mentors, family, personal discipline — reduce dependence. Dependence narrows vision. Diversification expands it.

Skills can also become a single basket.

Highly specialized expertise tied to one employer may pay well. But if that employer disappears, so does the opportunity. Portable skills are diversified skills.

Communication. Leadership. Sales. Negotiation. Problem-solving. Systems thinking.

These travel. And portability is leverage.

— — —

There is a deeper layer.

The skill, wealth vehicle, or education you pursue should not be single-use. It should be engineered.

Ask: Can this skill generate income in more than one environment? Can this certification apply across industries? Can this education create crossover opportunity?

A technical certification that only applies within one company's proprietary system is concentration.

A communication skill that improves leadership, sales, negotiation, and relationships simultaneously — that is diversification.

The asset may change. The knowledge remains.

— — —

There is a psychological resistance to diversification. It feels like spreading yourself thin. Like distraction. Like lack of focus.

But strategic diversification is not chaos. It is intentional distribution.

You do not need ten revenue streams. You need more than one.

You do not need ten identities. You need internal stability beyond title.

You do not need dozens of relationships. You need emotional resilience beyond one person.

Diversification does not eliminate risk. It reduces catastrophic exposure.

The goal is not to avoid commitment. It is to avoid structural dependence.

Commit fully. But build backup.

Invest deeply. But maintain portability.

Love fully. But maintain self-respect and independence.

Work hard. But develop alternatives.

— — —

Building Across Environments

Diversification that only works in one environment is concentration with extra steps.

This is a subtle but important distinction.

Consider someone who has built three income streams — but all three are within the same industry, serving the same client type, dependent on the same economic conditions. When that industry contracts, all three streams contract together. The diversification was structural only in appearance.

True diversification means building across environments — different industries, different client types, different economic drivers, different skill applications.

Here is a framework for assessing whether your diversification is genuine or correlated.

For each income stream or professional asset you possess, ask: What conditions would need to be true for this to fail significantly?

Then compare the conditions across your streams.

If the conditions overlap significantly — if the same recession, the same industry downturn, or the same technology shift would affect all of them simultaneously — you have correlated concentration.

If the conditions are genuinely different — if one stream might suffer while another is unaffected or even benefits — you have genuine diversification.

— — —

The Education Investment That Multiplies

I want to address education specifically, because it is one of the most significant financial and time investments most people make — and it is one of the areas where diversification thinking is most underapplied.

Most education is status-oriented rather than strategically engineered.

You pursue the qualification that looks impressive. The credential that signals participation in a recognised institution or profession. The degree that produces the title.

These have value. But the value is often less portable, less compounding, and more vulnerable than people realise.

Strategic education is engineered for crossover.

It asks: Does this knowledge apply across industries and environments, or only within one specific context?

Communication. Financial literacy. Leadership. Problem-solving frameworks. Systems thinking. Data interpretation. Negotiation. Sales.

These compound across every environment you will ever operate in. Every industry, every role, every relationship, every negotiation benefits from depth in these areas.

Technical certification specific to one employer's proprietary system does not.

When you invest time and money in education, ask: Where will this still be valuable in ten years? Across how many environments?

Invest in the answer to that question.

— — —

Reflection & Action

- What is my single largest basket?
- If that basket dropped, what would break?
- What skill could I develop that works across multiple industries?
- What income stream could I build outside my primary role?
- What part of my identity is overly tied to one environment?

Action — Add One Basket

Choose one or two:

- Begin building a secondary income stream
- Develop one portable, multi-use skill
- Invest in assets not tied to your employer
- Strengthen relationships outside your primary environment
- Pursue education engineered for crossover, not status

Diversification is not about excess.

It is about insulation.

And insulation creates leverage.

— — —

Diversification Reduces Dependence

What This Looks Like in Practice

The Diversification Blueprint is a practical roadmap for building resilience across the key areas of your life.

Most people approach diversification as something that happens in one domain — typically financial. But structural resilience requires distribution across multiple areas simultaneously.

Income Diversification

The goal: within 24 months, have at least two income sources, with the secondary source covering at least 15–20% of your essential monthly expenses.

Start by identifying one skill or area of knowledge you could offer as a service, consultation, or product. Then find the smallest viable first step — one client, one project, one piece of content — and execute it.

Do not wait until the secondary stream is substantial before starting. Start small and build. The psychology of having any secondary income is more valuable in the early stages than the income itself.

Skill Diversification

Map your current skills on two axes: Depth (how advanced is this skill?) and Portability (how transferable is this skill across industries and environments?).

High depth, low portability = specialisation risk. You are valuable but vulnerable.

High depth, high portability = optimal. Deep expertise that travels.

Low depth, high portability = foundational. These skills — communication, leadership, problem-solving, financial literacy — are worth developing even if they never become your primary expertise.

Invest in moving at least one skill from low portability to high portability within the next 12 months.

Identity Diversification

This one is underappreciated and worth spending time on.

Write down the top five answers you would give to the question: *Who am I?*

If the list is heavily dominated by your professional role — your title, your employer, your industry — you have identity concentration. When the role changes, you change with it more than is healthy.

Add to the list: roles you play outside work, values you hold, skills you possess, relationships you are part of. Build an identity that is distributed enough to remain intact when any single component changes.

— — —

The Diversification Mistake

There is a version of diversification that looks right and functions wrong.

It is when people diversify across areas that are all correlated — they spread across multiple things that would all fail simultaneously under the same disruption.

A salesperson who builds three income streams, all within the same industry. Appears diversified. But if that industry contracts, all three streams contract together.

A person who has three savings accounts but no additional income sources. Appears to have multiple financial structures. But all three depend on the same primary income.

Real diversification means the streams are non-correlated. When one is affected, the others are not.

Ask yourself: if my primary income stream experienced a major disruption — not just slowed, but stopped — how many of my other streams would survive unaffected?

If the answer is none, you have correlated concentration, not genuine diversification.

Build streams that survive different kinds of disruption. Different industries. Different skill sets. Different income mechanisms. Different client bases.

That is the diversification that actually reduces dependence.

— — —

CODE 9

Calm Is Leverage

Two people walk into the same negotiation.

Same numbers. Same opportunity. Same pressure.

One speaks quickly. Explains too much. Fills every silence. Justifies their position repeatedly. Moves fast.

The other pauses. Listens. Lets silence stretch. Responds slowly. Does not rush.

Same information. Different outcome.

Calm is leverage.

— — —

Pressure reveals structure.

When you operate from need, pressure accelerates your speech, shortens your thinking, and increases your concession rate. You want the deal. You want the approval. You want the reassurance.

So you move faster. And speed under pressure is often weakness dressed as confidence.

The calm person is not necessarily smarter. They are insulated.

They can wait. Waiting creates power. Silence creates tension. The person who can tolerate silence controls the rhythm. The person who controls the rhythm controls the outcome.

— — —

Calm is not personality. It is structure.

If losing the deal would not destabilize your life, your nervous system behaves differently. If losing the job would not collapse your situation, your voice stays steady. If walking away is survivable, your breathing stays even.

Calm is often backed by math.

In negotiation, desperation is visible — even when unspoken. Micro-expressions. Tone shifts. Over-explaining. Immediate concessions. Pressure leaks.

Experienced negotiators sense it immediately.

Calm does the opposite. It signals options. It signals insulation. It signals position.

This is not about suppressing emotion. It is about regulating it. Regulation creates clarity. Clarity improves decisions. Better decisions compound. Leverage compounds.

— — —

Consider two investors during a market drop.

One checks their account every hour. Sells early. Locks in the loss.

The other reviews their plan. Rebalances calmly. Executes deliberately.

Same market. Different nervous system.

Calm preserved leverage. Panic surrendered it.

— — —

Calm is also powerful in conflict.

When someone raises their voice and you do not. When someone pressures and you pause. When someone demands and you say, "Let me think about that."

That pause shifts power. Because urgency transfers. The calmer party absorbs less pressure. The reactive party absorbs more.

But here is the honest part: calm is not natural when you are exposed.

If you are one paycheck from collapse, your body knows it. If one outcome determines your survival, your brain accelerates. You cannot fake calm sustainably.

You build it.

Through savings. Reduced obligations. Diversification. Skill portability. Clear boundaries.

Structure stabilizes the nervous system.

— — —

There is a reason highly positioned people appear patient. They are not immune to stress. They are insulated from collapse. Remove collapse fear, and composure rises.

If you want calm, reduce fragility.

If you want composure, increase options.

If you want negotiating power, build insulation.

You cannot will yourself into calm while structurally exposed.

You engineer calm.

— — —

Here is a practical test.

The next time you are in a high-pressure conversation: slow your speech by 10%. Pause before answering. Let silence sit for three seconds longer than feels comfortable.

Observe what happens.

Often, the other person fills the space. And in filling it, they reveal leverage.

Calm does not mean passive. It means controlled. It means deliberate. It means you are not operating from fear.

Fear accelerates. Leverage slows.

In moments of disruption, calm separates survivors from casualties. Not because calm prevents loss. Because calm prevents mistakes under pressure. And mistakes under pressure are expensive.

You do not need to be intimidating.

You need to be steady.

Steadiness creates gravity. Gravity creates influence. Influence is leverage.

— — —

Calm in the High-Stakes Moments

I want to walk through a specific high-stakes situation where calm leverage plays out in real time — because abstract descriptions of calm only go so far.

Imagine you are in a performance review. Your manager opens by framing your performance as solid but below expectations in a specific area. The framing is accurate in some ways, unfair in others. You feel the instinct to respond immediately — to correct, to defend, to explain.

The undisciplined response: you speak quickly, over-explain, justify, become slightly defensive. The conversation has an emotional charge. Your manager retains control of the framing. The outcome reflects their initial assessment more than your actual contribution.

The positioned response: you pause. You let the framing sit for a moment without immediately filling the space. Then you respond deliberately.

"I appreciate the feedback. I want to make sure I understand the specific concerns before I respond. Can you walk me through the examples you are thinking of?"

This response does three things simultaneously.

It buys time — allowing you to think rather than react.

It requests specificity — which often reveals that the original framing was more general than precise.

It signals calm — communicating to your manager that you are not destabilized, which shifts the power dynamic of the conversation.

From that position, you can engage substantively with the specific examples rather than broadly defending against a general framing. The conversation becomes more factual, less emotional. Your preparation and actual performance become more visible.

You may or may not change the outcome of the review. But you have changed the quality of the conversation — and over time, the consistent experience of engaging with you from a position of calm and precision changes how you are perceived and treated.

— — —

The Silence Experiment

Here is a practical exercise I want you to try in the next seven days.

In at least three conversations — professional or personal — deliberately hold silence for three to four seconds after the other person finishes speaking before you respond.

Not aggressively. Not theatrically. Simply as a consistent practice.

Notice what happens.

In most cases, one of two things occurs.

The other person adds to what they said — revealing more than they initially shared. This is information you would not have had if you had responded immediately.

Or the silence creates a brief moment of recalibration — both parties pause before proceeding. The conversation slows slightly. The quality of what follows tends to improve.

The second thing to notice is what happens inside you.

Most people find that the first time or two, the silence feels acutely uncomfortable. The urge to fill it is almost physical.

But with practice, the discomfort fades. And what replaces it is something valuable: the experience of not being driven by the discomfort of silence. Of being the person who sets the pace rather than the person who reacts to it.

That experience — small, private, repeated — is the beginning of practised calm.

And practised calm, over time, is leverage.

— — —

Reflection & Action

- When pressured, do I speed up or slow down?
- What situations trigger urgency in me?
- Is that urgency emotional — or structural?
- If I had six months of expenses saved, how would I behave differently?
- Where does fear distort my communication?

Action — Train Calm

Choose one or two:

- Practice pausing before responding in negotiations
- Build savings to reduce fear of collapse
- Reduce one dependency that increases urgency
- Train physical regulation — breathing, fitness, sleep
- Delay decisions when emotionally elevated

Calm is not gifted.

It is built.

And built calm is leverage.

— — —

Calm Is Leverage

What This Looks Like in Practice

Calm under pressure is not a personality trait. It is a trainable capacity — and like all trainable capacities, it improves with deliberate practice.

Here is the Calm Practice Framework, built around three levels of training.

Level 1: Physical Regulation

The body responds to threat before the mind does. When you feel pressure rising in a conversation or situation, your heart rate increases, your breathing shallows, your thinking narrows.

The fastest way to interrupt this physiological response is controlled breathing.

Specifically: inhale for four counts, hold for four counts, exhale for six counts. This activates the parasympathetic nervous system and physically interrupts the stress response within 60–90 seconds.

Practice this daily — not just in high-pressure moments, but as a regular discipline. The people who can access physical calm under pressure are the ones who have practised it when there was no pressure, until it becomes automatic.

Level 2: The Pause Habit

In conversations, practice the deliberate pause before responding.

Not a theatrical pause. Not silence as a power move. Simply the habit of taking two to three seconds before you respond to anything — a question, an offer, a challenge.

This does one thing more than anything else: it prevents reactive responding.

Most poor decisions in negotiations and conversations happen in the first three seconds. The pause eliminates that window.

Practise this in low-stakes conversations first. Build the habit before you need it in high-stakes ones.

Level 3: Structural Calm

This is the foundation beneath the other two.

Sustainable calm under pressure is not primarily a breathing technique or a communication habit. It is structural insulation.

The person who has three months of savings breathes differently in a performance review than the person who has none. Not because they have practised more. Because the stakes of the conversation are structurally different.

Every structural improvement you make — savings built, dependency reduced, option added — increases your natural calm under pressure.

You are not engineering a feeling. You are engineering the conditions that produce the feeling.

— — —

Calm in a Real Conversation

I want to give you a specific example of what practiced calm looks like in a real negotiation — not a theoretical one.

Several years ago, I was in a contract conversation that felt heavily weighted toward the other party. They had set the terms. They had set the timeline. They had framed it as essentially settled.

The old version of me would have accepted quickly — not because the terms were right, but because the discomfort of resistance felt too costly.

Instead, I paused.

Not dramatically. I simply said: *"I want to make sure I understand all of this properly before I respond. Can I come back to you in two days?"*

They were surprised. Not offended — surprised. They had expected an immediate answer.

In those two days, I assessed the terms clearly. I identified three specific areas I was not comfortable with. I determined what I would accept, what I would not, and what I was willing to walk away from.

When I returned, I was calm. Not aggressive. Not apologetic.

"I've had time to look at this carefully. There are three areas I'd like to discuss before we finalize anything."

The conversation that followed was the best negotiation I have had. Not because I won everything I wanted. Because I negotiated from clarity rather than from discomfort.

The two-day pause was not a tactic.

It was structure.

— — —

CODE 10

You Do Not Need to Look Powerful. You Need to Be Positioned.

The world rewards appearance.

Titles. Cars. Announcements. Upgrades. Recognition.

It applauds visibility.

But visibility is not leverage.

Position is leverage. And position is rarely visible.

— — —

Many people spend their energy looking powerful.

Projecting success. Signaling lifestyle. Broadcasting momentum. They upgrade before insulating. They expand before stabilizing. They display before engineering.

And when disruption arrives, the projection collapses.

Because projection is performance. Position is structure.

Power can be rented. Position must be built.

Power can be granted, taken away, and reassigned. Position compounds quietly.

Power depends on perception. Position depends on math.

— — —

You can look powerful and be fragile.

You can look ordinary and be insulated.

One collapses under pressure. The other absorbs it.

This is the uncomfortable truth: most people are optimizing for how their life looks. Very few are optimizing for how their life holds.

Leverage is not about optics. It is about endurance.

The executive with a high income and no savings is exposed.

The entrepreneur with one large client is exposed.

The partner emotionally dependent on one outcome is exposed.

They may look strong. But they are concentrated. And concentration is fragility wearing confidence.

— — —

Position means:

If income stops, you adjust.

If a deal falls through, you pivot.

If someone leaves, you remain intact.

If pressure rises, you do not panic.

That is leverage.

You do not need to dominate rooms. You need to withstand storms.

You do not need to signal status. You need to protect structure.

You do not need applause. You need insulation.

— — —

There will always be someone louder. Someone flashier. Someone more visible. Someone projecting more success.

Let them.

Because when cycles shift — and they always do — visibility fades quickly.

Structure always wins.

If you are chasing image over insulation, you are building vulnerability.

If you are building insulation over image, you are building leverage.

Choose carefully.

— — —

Leverage is not accidental. It is engineered.

It is built within savings accounts, reduced fixed costs, multi-use skills, diversified income, emotional discipline, and calm under pressure.

Layer by layer. Quietly. Intentionally.

You do not need to look powerful.

You need to be positioned.

Positioning is not glamorous. It is disciplined. It is patient. It is deliberate. It is often invisible.

But it wins.

When life disrupts you — and it will — you will not scramble. You will not collapse. You will not negotiate from fear.

You will steady yourself. You will assess. You will decide.

Because you are not operating from need.

You are operating from position.

Life is not equal. It is all about leverage.

Some build appearance. Others build structure.

Build structure. As often and as deliberately as possible.

— — —

The Person You Are Building Toward

I want to end this book with a specific kind of question.

Not a reflection question. Not an action item. A vision question.

Imagine yourself five years from now. Not the impressive version — not the version with the title or the status or the visible achievements.

The positioned version.

The version of you who has spent the past five years building quietly. Who has savings that provide genuine breathing room. Who has reduced fixed obligations to a level that no longer creates constant background pressure. Who has developed skills that are portable, monetizable, and genuinely valued across more than one environment. Who has secondary income that does not depend entirely on one employer's continued approval.

Who has — in the language of this book — built the invisible you to a level where the visible you can afford to be honest, patient, and genuinely selective.

How does that person walk into a negotiation?

How does that person respond to disruption?

How does that person handle pressure?

How does that person make decisions about time, money, relationships, and direction?

Now ask: What is the distance between where you are now and that version of you?

And what is the single most important thing you could do this week to begin closing it?

That question — answered honestly, acted on consistently — is the entire work of this book in practice.

— — —

The Two Things That Change

I have been thinking about leverage for a long time now. Lived without it, scrambled toward it, built it gradually, lost some of it, rebuilt it again.

Here is what I know for certain.

Two things change when you build genuine structural leverage.

The first is external. You get better outcomes. Better negotiations. More stability through disruption. More options in decisions. More freedom in choices. The math of your life improves.

But the second thing — and I believe this is ultimately more important — is internal.

You stop operating from fear.

Not completely. Not permanently. Fear is part of being human, and anyone who claims otherwise is either unusually fortunate or not being honest.

But the specific fear of collapse — the fear that one wrong move, one missed deposit, one bad piece of news will unravel everything — that fear diminishes.

And when that fear diminishes, something opens up.

Clarity. The ability to think longer-term. The capacity to be generous rather than defensive. The willingness to take considered risks rather than staying frozen in false security.

The fear of collapse is one of the most expensive things most people carry. It distorts decisions. It narrows vision. It keeps people in situations they should leave, and out of situations they should enter.

Building leverage does not eliminate all fear. But it addresses the structural root of the fear that costs the most.

That is worth building for.

Not just for the outcomes it produces — though those are real and significant.

For the freedom it creates inside.

— — —

Reflection & Action

- Where am I projecting strength instead of building it?
- What visible upgrade have I prioritized over insulation?
- If disruption hit tomorrow, would my image matter — or my structure?
- What one structural improvement would change my posture immediately?

Action — Choose Position

Choose one or two:

- Increase margin before increasing lifestyle
- Build one skill that compounds across environments
- Reduce one dependency quietly
- Strengthen one boundary without announcing it
- Track structure, not status

You do not need to look powerful.

You need to be positioned.

Build accordingly.

— — —

You Do Not Need to Look Powerful. You Need to Be Positioned.

What This Looks Like in Practice

The Position vs. Appearance Audit is a final, comprehensive exercise that brings together everything in this book.

For each area below, give yourself two scores from 1 to 5:

First score: How strong is the **appearance** of strength in this area?

Second score: How strong is the **actual structural position** in this area?

Financial:

Appearance: Do you look financially stable to others?

Position: Do you have savings, low fixed costs, and income diversification?

Career:

Appearance: Do you have an impressive title, visible achievements, a strong profile?

Position: Do you have portable skills, alternatives, and negotiating leverage?

Relationships:

Appearance: Do your relationships appear healthy and strong from the outside?

Position: Are your relationships genuinely chosen — or held together by dependency?

Health:

Appearance: Do you present as healthy and capable?

Position: Is your physical and mental health genuinely strong enough to absorb sustained pressure?

Now compare the two scores in each area.

Where appearance significantly exceeds position, you are carrying structural risk. You are projecting strength you have not yet built.

Where position meets or exceeds appearance, you have genuine leverage.

This gap — between what you project and what you possess — is the most important number in this book.

Spend the next year closing it.

— — —

The Long Game

This is the final thing I want to say, and I want to say it plainly.

Building leverage is a long game.

It is not a weekend project. It is not a single decision. It is not a moment of inspiration followed by transformation.

It is a series of quiet, uncelebrated decisions made consistently over months and years.

Savings built when spending felt more satisfying.

Fixed costs reduced when maintaining them felt easier.

Skills developed when rest would have been more comfortable.

Boundaries held when dissolving them would have avoided conflict.

Options built before they were needed.

None of it glamorous. All of it structural.

I think about the version of myself who lay awake running numbers after that cost-cutting email. Who sat across from a paycheck that looked fine and felt thin. Who experienced the compression of disruption without a parachute.

I was not a different person than I am now.

I was the same person, in different structural circumstances.

The difference between those two versions of me is not wisdom or willpower or some transformation of character.

It is positioning.

Quiet, patient, deliberate positioning built over time.

The world will continue to reward appearance. Visibility will continue to attract attention. The loudest and most visible version of success will continue to get the most applause.

Let it.

Build the invisible version.

Build structure before you need it.

Build leverage before disruption arrives to test it.

And over time — not quickly, but certainly — you will feel the difference between operating from need and operating from position.

That difference is worth every quiet, uncelebrated decision it took to build.

— — —

Closing: Build With Intention

You now understand the mechanics.

Leverage is not personality, status, or performance. It is structure. Insulation. Options. Discipline. Calm under pressure. Diversified strength. Invisible preparation.

You do not build leverage once. You build it repeatedly. Intentionally.

Every decision is either increasing your position — or weakening it. Every expense. Every commitment. Every skill pursued. Every boundary set. Every hour invested.

Some decisions increase margin. Some increase exposure. Some expand options. Some narrow them.

You may not see the difference immediately. But you will feel it over time.

— — —

Before you upgrade, ask: Does this strengthen my position?

Before you commit, ask: Does this increase my leverage — or my dependency?

Before you react, ask: Am I operating from need — or from structure?

These questions are small. Their impact compounds.

— — —

Leverage does not require perfection. It requires awareness. You will still enjoy life. Still spend. Still commit. Still risk.

But you will do it strategically.

Build margin first. Insulation first. Options first. Then expansion.

Try it.

Increase your savings rate for six months. Reduce one fixed obligation. Develop one portable skill. Build one additional income stream. Strengthen one boundary. Pause longer in negotiation. Delay one upgrade. Build structure quietly.

You will feel the difference. You will breathe differently. You will negotiate differently. You will respond differently.

Because you are not operating from need.

You are operating from position.

— — —

The world will continue to reward visibility. That will not change.

But life rewards stability. That does not change either.

When disruption comes — and it will — you will not scramble for identity. You will not negotiate from fear. You will not collapse under pressure.

You will steady yourself.

Because you built structure before you needed it.

Life is not equal.

It is all about leverage.

Some drift into dependence. Some build position.

Choose deliberately. Build with intention. Build structure. Build leverage.

As often as possible.

And over time, you will experience the difference.

— — —

About the Author

MJ Carver writes about leverage, positioning, relationships, and structural freedom in life and work.

Drawing from professional leadership experience spanning corporate environments, process improvement, and personal disruption, his work focuses on building margin, reducing fragility, strengthening position, and increasing options in an uncertain world.

The Leverage Code is the foundational book in a broader philosophy centered on intentional structure and long-term positioning. It is followed by *Love, Positioned* and *Spat-Out.*

— — —

Continue Building

If this book challenged you, strengthened you, or shifted how you think about leverage, do not stop here.

Leverage compounds. Positioning compounds. Structure compounds.

The ideas in this book are part of a broader framework focused on building margin, reducing fragility, and expanding options in life and work. If you are interested in learning more, email me at mjmj2222@gmail.com

Or; join my mailing list on my website: www.mjcarverbooks.com

I will send you an update on a new community focused on "The Life Strategy Series" — along with book updates and digital resources as they become available.

Build quietly.

Position deliberately.

Stay insulated.

Because options are freedom.— — —

Other Books By MJ Carver

LOVE, POSITIONED — Falling In Love Is Not A Strategy

SPAT-OUT — When Profits Over People Affects You

www.ingramcontent.com/pod-product-compliance
Lightning Source LLC
LaVergne TN
LVHW012055160826
845678LV00014B/2837

9798995424512